AMERICAN EASTERN CATHOLICS

PASTORAL SPIRITUALITY SERIES

AMERICAN EASTERN CATHOLICS

by
Fred J. Saato

Paulist Press
New York/Mahwah, NJ

"Appendix of Differences between the Eastern and Western Churches" used by permission of Andriy Chirovsky, Metropolitan Andrey Sheptytsky Institute of Eastern Christian Studies, Saint Paul University, Ottawa, Canada.

Appendix B, "A Comparison of Two Traditions" adapted with permission from Andriy Chirovsky, *Two Different Traditions—One Catholic Church, Different—Yet the Same* and *When Thinking of Major Catholic Doctrines* (Ottawa: Metropolitan Andrey Sheptytsky Institute of Eastern Christian Studies, Saint Paul University, 1999).

The Scripture quotations contained herein are from the New Revised Standard Version: Catholic Edition Copyright © 1989 and 1993, by the Division of Christian Education of the National Council of the Churches of Christ in the United States of America. Used by permission. All rights reserved.

Extracts from the Documents of the Second Vatican Council are the author's translation and from Walter Abbot's edition of *The Documents of Vatican II* © 1966 by America Press used by kind permission of America Press. Visit: www.americamagazine.org.

Cover design by Trudi Gershenov
Book design by Lynn Else

Library of Congress Cataloging-in-Publication Data

Saato, Fred J.
    American eastern Catholics / by Fred J. Saato.
        p.   cm. — (Pastoral spirituality series)
    Includes bibliographical references.
    ISBN 0-8091-4378-X (alk. paper)
    1. Catholic Church—Oriental rites—United States—History. 2. United States—Church history. I. Title. II. Series.
BX4710.35.S23 2006
281'.5—dc22

                                                                    2006021815

Published by Paulist Press
997 Macarthur Boulevard
Mahwah, New Jersey 07430

www.paulistpress.com

Printed and bound in the
United States of America

CONTENTS

CONTENTS

To the Reverend Father Austin P. Mohrbacher
who made so many aware of the Eastern Churches
and who inspired many to strive for the
union of the Churches

INTRODUCTION
TO THE SERIES

The American Catholic Church is an "institutional immigrant" composed of many racial and ethnic groups with diverse religious and cultural traditions. Earlier groups, mostly of Western European countries, have by and large moved into the mainstream of American society and currently constitute the majority of American Catholics. Recent immigrants and refugees come from other parts of the world, such as Asia, the Caribbean Islands, Eastern Europe, and Latin America. Together with the original native people who were present on the continent before the so-called discovery of the New World, these newcomers have dramatically swelled the ranks of the American Catholic Church. The native peoples and these newer immigrants and refugees—both documented and undocumented—are in many ways a blessing and boon for the American society and the American Catholic Church. Recently the U.S. Conference of Catholic Bishops (USCCB) has recognized the importance and contributions of these peoples in two statements, *Welcoming the Stranger Among Us: Unity in Diversity* (2000) and *Asian and Pacific Presence: Harmony in Faith* (2001). At the same time, both American society and the Church are facing difficult challenges with regard to these people who are, culturally and religiously, different from their European predecessors and quite diverse among themselves. Part of the difficulty lies in the absence of up-to-date and accurate information on these ethnic groups and their cultural and religious backgrounds.

To help the Catholic Church in the United States carry out its pastoral ministry to all people, Paulist Press, in collaboration with Daniel Mullhall, the Assistant Secretary for Catechesis and Inculturation at the U.S. Conference of Catholic Bishops, is issuing this series of books on the cultural and religious heritages of many of these ethnic groups. The ultimate aim of these books is to promote communion in the Church, a communion that recognizes and celebrates the diversity of God's blessings in the ethnic, racial, sociopolitical, sexual, religious, and cultural richness that all peoples bring to the United States. Such a communion eschews uniformity, and yet seeks to maintain and develop the unity in faith, hope, and love in the service of God's reign.

The publisher, authors, and editors of this series fervently hope that these books will contribute to a better understanding of and appreciation for the unique cultural and religious heritages these communities bring with them to share with the church in the United States. In the long run, their presence will forge a new type of America and a new model of Church.

Peter C. Phan
Series General Editor

PREFACE
WHAT IS A CATHOLIC CHURCH?

I could not have been more than eight or nine years old when I first heard the Lord's words recorded in Matthew 16:18: "On this rock I will build my church." I couldn't get over my good fortune that the church Jesus built (obviously my parish church) and the rock it was built upon (its rugged cornerstone) were only two blocks from my house! I knew what a church was and what a rock was—my reasoning was flawless!

I was not the first person to reach a flawed conclusion based on a limited experience of the matter at hand, nor would I be the last. The experience of most American Catholics is that "the Catholic Church" equals the *Roman* Catholic Church, which they know. Many older Catholics may remember hearing how the Mass they knew from their parish church was celebrated the same way all over the world. This demonstrated the Church's universality.

While Western thought tends to focus on the universal Church, Eastern authors prefer to stress another concept: that the fullness of the Church is found in the local Church (diocese or eparchy) in communion with its sister Churches. This fullness is particularly evident in the Eucharistic assembly at which bishop, clergy, and laity are united at the holy table. The aim of this volume is to stress this aspect of this Mystery of the Body of Christ: that there are in fact *several* Catholic Churches in the United States. They are in communion with one another, but are not necessarily united structurally in the same way. They have different theologies, different liturgies, different spiritualities, different hierarchies and disciplines. Each is complete and distinct in its own way; yet each would be incomplete somehow if it were not in communion with others.

A "Universal Church" or a Communion of Churches?

The other groups, to which volumes in this series are devoted, are indeed many faces of one Catholic Church in the United States: the Roman Church. People of many ethnic groups have emigrated from different countries or embody the values of different cultures, but they are all part of one particular Catholic Church: the Latin Church. This book examines some of the other members of the Catholic "body of Churches"[1] established in this country: the Eastern Catholic Churches. They may be tied to one or another of the Eastern Patriarchates or even be autonomous *(sui juris)*. Some aspects of their traditions complement Western practice; others seem to contradict it. It is this very dynamic that, while incomprehensible to some, can give us a greater insight into the heart of what it means to be a Church in the communion of the Holy Spirit.

These initial remarks about Catholic Church versus Catholic Churches may illustrate the point. Both approaches are found in the New Testament. Saint Paul sees the Church first of all as the local assembly (for example, referring to "all the churches of the saints," 1 Cor 14:33), which is the Body of Christ. In the East, "the one, holy, catholic and apostolic Church" would basically mean what today may be called the "diocese": the gathering of believers led by their bishop, assisted by his priests and deacons,[2] living the fullness of the sacramental life in Christ. Each local Church would be Catholic (whole and complete) and exist in a communion of faith with others through their bishop.

Over the centuries subsequent structures such as *metropolias* or patriarchates were established to foster unity. These became the focal points for the development of specific liturgical and spiritual traditions that would be made concrete in the local Church, the prime experience of the Body of Christ in the authentic tradition of the Christian East. As the late Byzantine Catholic Metropolitan of Pittsburgh reminded the bishops gathered at the Synod for the Americas in 1997, "The universal Church is, in fact, a communion of Churches with their own theology, liturgy, spirituality and discipline which do not contradict but complement one another."[3]

Other New Testament writings, however, speak of the Church in more universal terms (see Ephesians and Colossians as well as the verse in Matthew cited previously). This would contribute to the ever-increasing centralization of the Roman Church, culminating in the vision of the First Vatican Council and the resulting structures characterizing the twentieth-century Church.

In fact, the Church is complete and the Body of Christ in both local and universal aspects. Each vision can express something of the Mystery of the Church; yet each is also susceptible to distortion. A universalist idea of the Church has often led to a kind of imperialism on the part of popes and patriarchs. A localized vision of the Church can often reduce the Body of Christ to an ethnic or political social club. Both dimensions, complementing one another, are required to convey the deeper reality. It is the particular gift of the Eastern Catholic Churches today to manifest this diversity in the West for the sake of all the Churches. This volume attempts to describe the various Eastern Catholic Churches in North America, some important characteristics of their traditions, and how the wider Catholic and Christian families can profit from the presence of these Churches in their midst.

The Eastern Catholic Churches in North America

At this writing, the following ten Eastern Catholic Churches have been established in the United States and Canada:

1. *The Armenian Catholic Church,* derived from the Armenian Catholicate of Cilicia with one eparchy headquartered in Brooklyn, New York, serving both Canada and the United States.

2. *The Chaldean Catholic Church,* derived from and connected to the Assyro-Chaldean Patriarchate in Baghdad, Iraq; with eparchies in Southfield, Michigan, and El Cajon, California, for the United States.

3. *The Maronite Church,* derived from and connected to the Maronite Patriarchal Church of Antioch and all the East; with eparchies in Brooklyn, New York; St. Louis, Missouri; and Montreal, Quebec, for the United States and Canada respectively.

4. *The Melkite Greek Catholic Church* (the Byzantine Church of the Middle East), derived from and connected to the Patriarchate of Antioch and all the East; with eparchies in Newton, Massachusetts, and Montreal, Quebec, for the United States and Canada respectively.

5. *The Romanian Greek Catholic Church,* derived from the Greek Catholic Metropolia of Alba Julia and Fagaras in Romania, with one eparchy in Canton, Ohio, for the United States; in Canada, the Romanian exarchate is part of the Ukrainian Metropolia.

6. *The Ruthenian Byzantine Catholic Church,* derived from the Greek Catholic Church in the former Austro-Hungarian Empire. An autonomous *(sui juris)* Church with an archeparchy in Pittsburgh, Pennsylvania, and eparchies in Passaic, New Jersey; Parma, Ohio; and Van Nuys, California. In Canada, this Church is called Slovak, from the present-day nation from which many of its members emigrated. It is headquartered in Unionville, Ontario.

7. *The Syriac Catholic Church,* derived from and connected to the Syriac Patriarchate of Antioch and all the East; with an eparchy in Union City, New Jersey, serving parishes in both the United States and Canada.

8. *The Syro-Malabar Catholic Church,* derived from and connected to the Syro-Malabar Church in India, with an eparchy for the United States in Cicero, Illinois. Called the *Mar Thoma Nazranikal* (Nazarenes of St. Thomas), this Church was "renamed" by the Vatican in the nineteenth century. Recently the bishops of this Church have introduced a version of the earlier name, "Church of the St. Thomas Christians." Integrated into this eparchy is the "Southist," or "Knanaya" Mission. According to tradition, the Knanaya can be traced to a group of seventy-two Jewish Christian families who immigrated to India from Mesopotamia in AD 345. The bishop also serves as permanent visitor for Syro-Malabar parishes in Canada.

9. *The Syro-Malankara Catholic Church,* derived from and connected to the (West) Syrian Church in India, with a mission centered in New Hyde Park, New York, and supervised by a bishop from the Church in India, coordinating parishes in the United States and Canada.

10. *The Ukrainian Greek Catholic Church*, derived from and connected to the Metropolia of Kiev and Halych, the Greek Catholic Church in Poland and Ukraine. It consists of a metropolia in Canada (Winnipeg, Manitoba, with suffragan eparchies in Edmonton, Alberta; New Westminster, British Columbia; Toronto, Ontario; and Saskatoon, Saskatchewan) and another in the United States (Philadelphia, Pennsylvania, with suffragan eparchies in Chicago, Illinois; Parma, Ohio; and Stamford, Connecticut).

Contact information for these jurisdictions may be found in Appendix A.

In addition, scattered parishes from other Eastern Catholic Churches (Coptic, Ethiopian, Italo-Greek, and Russian Greek Catholic) are administered by local Roman or Eastern Catholic bishops.

The Orthodox and Other Eastern Churches

At the same time, it must not be forgotten that these Eastern Catholic Churches represent a minority of the Eastern Churches in the United States and throughout the world. Except for the Armenian Apostolic Church and the Assyrian Church of the East, most use the title *Orthodox* along with a reference to their ethnic and spiritual background (for example, Albanian or Coptic Orthodox). Sadly, these Churches are *not* in communion with all of the others or with the West. There are currently three communions of Eastern Churches based on these divisions of the first millennium, all of which have dioceses in the West:

1. *The Church of the East:* This Church was separated from the rest of the Christian world after the Council of Ephesus (431). It follows the East Syrian tradition,

as do the Chaldean and Syro-Malabar Catholics. Members of this Church in the United States are chiefly Assyrians who emigrated from Iran and Iraq or from southern India.

2. *The Oriental Orthodox Churches:* The Armenian, Coptic, Eritrean, Ethiopian, Indian, and Syrian Orthodox Churches belong to this communion, although they represent three distinct traditions. The Copts and Syrians were separated from the Greek and Latin Churches after the Council of Chalcedon (451) and were later joined by the Armenians.

3. *The Eastern Orthodox Churches:* This term is used by the Orthodox Churches following the tradition of the Greek Fathers and employing the Byzantine rite (for example, Albanians, Greeks, Russians, Ukrainians, and so on). A variety of issues at the end of the first Christian millennium periodically divided the Greek and Latin Churches. This division became fixed due to the way Western nations treated the Orthodox during the Crusades and the Turkish invasion of the Byzantine Empire, as well as the development of doctrine in the Western Church during the second millennium.

Canonical Eastern Orthodox Churches (those connected to mother Churches in Europe, Asia, and Africa) are members of the Standing Conference of Orthodox Bishops in America (SCOBA). Canonical Oriental Orthodox Churches are members of the Standing Conference of Oriental Orthodox Churches (SCOOCH).

While the Roman Catholic Church has consistently refused the title *Church* to any Protestant denomination, it refers to all the historic Eastern Churches as "sister Churches." While Protestant communities have set aside elements of historic Church practice, particularly the sacraments, the Orthodox and other Eastern Churches have maintained them unwaveringly, rejecting nothing of the life and faith of early Christianity. Rome recognizes them as sister Churches because they have maintained the faith of the Apostolic Church as expressed in the Nicene Creed and the sacramental life of the undivided Church over the centuries, despite theological differences that arose later and that divided them from one another. This is why the Roman Catholic Church recognizes the priesthood and sacraments of these Churches and longs for the day when communion can be reestablished with them.

For the greater part of their history, the Eastern Catholic Churches were part of these other Eastern Churches and in many ways have a greater spiritual kinship with them than with the Roman Catholic Church. In the same way, Roman Catholics may feel more at home at an Episcopal or Lutheran service than at an Eastern Catholic liturgy. The challenge to members of all the historic Churches, Eastern and Western, is to see what is truly Catholic and Apostolic in all our traditions. The annual *Orientale Lumen* Conferences at Washington's Catholic University have been important occasions for bringing members of all these Churches together and have resulted in the convocation of similar gatherings in other parts of the world.

Notes

1. Second Vatican Council, Dogmatic Constitution on the Church, *Lumen Gentium*, no. 23.
2. See the Letters of Saint Ignatius of Antioch.
3. *Servizio Informazioni Chiese Orientali* Bulletin (Rome: Congregation for the Eastern Churches, 1997), 12.

Chapter 1

A BIT OF HISTORY

THE TWO THOUSAND YEARS OF EASTERN CHRISTIANITY

American schools have long been known for their provincial approach to the world in which we live. Growing up in Brooklyn, New York, I was regularly taught about the local battles in the American Revolutionary War and how the Industrial Revolution affected New York cities like Schenectady and Watervliet. I never heard anything about ancient cultures or even the history of the modern world. My father, who had attended a French school in the Middle East, could never understand this.

A similar kind of tunnel vision affects our perception of Church history. The climactic events of Eastern history—the Christological conflicts, iconoclasm, and the Fourth Crusade—are vague memories for the Western Church. Western Christians, on the other hand, are used to seeing the sixteenth-century Reformation as the watershed experience in the history of the entire Church. Protestants point to it as the time in which the Church was renewed; Roman Catholics see at as the era in which the Protestant denominations came into being and the Council of Trent set the course of modern Catholic history. Eastern Christians, who were not a party to this upheaval, see these events as particular to the Western Church, a footnote in the history of the Christian era, which would have only negative effects on them. What are the most important milestones in Church history for Eastern Christians?

A. The First Millennium

1. We Were There at the Beginning

First of all, Eastern Christians feel closely connected with the beginnings of the Church. Christianity is an "Eastern religion." It originated with the Jewish and Gentile Semites of Galilee and Judea who followed Christ. Its first center would be Jerusalem, still called "Mother of All the Churches" in the Christian East today. The term *Christian* would be used first in Antioch (Acts 11:26), a Greek-speaking center of Hellenistic culture, which was the capital of "the East," a province of the Roman Empire embracing many contemporary nations in the Middle East, from Turkey to Jordan. The first Christian centers of note would be in the cities of the eastern part of the empire, along the Mediterranean and Adriatic coasts. The first great Christian missions would be the outreach of the Syrian Churches in Asia. The so-called Thomas Christians of Kerala (Syro-Malabar and Syro-Malankara Catholics, Malankara Syrian Orthodox, Mar Thoma Church, and the Church of the East) are the living descendants of these ancient missions. The great Christian strongholds of Western Europe would not develop until centuries later and would not outshine Constantinople, capital of the Eastern Empire, until its fall to the Turks in the mid-fifteenth century.

2. We've Been There Ever Since

For fifteen out of the twenty centuries of Christian history, the primary focus of the Church's activity was in the East. Our schools, unfortunately, barely acquaint us with the history of Western Europe and completely ignore the East, as if the first millennium of the Church's history did not exist. Many Eastern Christians contend that it is this first millennium that presents a vision of the Church more faithful to the Scriptures and the Fathers than the second. Subjection to Islamic rule would curtail the Eastern Churches' outward activities, including missionary activity, but it would also help the Eastern Churches keep their focus on the priorities of the patristic era and preserve what would be a surprisingly contemporary vision for the Church today.

3. The "Conversion" of Rome

A series of upheavals affected the Christian East, many of which still impact these Churches today. Seen as most climactic are the Christianization of the Roman Empire and the relocation of its capital from the Old Rome (in Italy) to the New Rome (Constantinople). This process began in AD 312, when Constantine the Great saw a vision of the cross in the sky accompanied by the words, *In this sign conquer.* During the next twenty-five years, Constantine ended the persecution of Christians, gave recognition and favors to the Church, established a new Christian capital far from the pagan associations of Old Rome, saw to the revival and adornment of Jerusalem with a host of shrines and churches, and summoned the first Ecumenical Council to unify the Church's faith amid the Arian controversy.

Greek (Byzantine) Christians consider Constantine the Great and his mother Helena not only saints but "Equals to the Apostles" for their part in these events. Constantine's vision is the inspiration behind the inscription on Byzantine Eucharistic breads: a cross and the words "Jesus Christ conquers."

4. *Did You Say Apostolic* Sees?

Although Constantine's empire was to continue in Eastern Europe and Asia Minor for more than eleven hundred years, it is the church structure his bishops established that survives in the consciousness of the Eastern Churches today. During the first three centuries of the Christian era, church organization was minimal due to the intermittent persecutions to which Christians were subjected. Even then Churches in villages and rural areas tended to follow the lead of the Churches in the principal cities of the area. This would give rise to what we might call "archdioceses," several local Churches maintaining their unity by dependence upon a local primate.

Constantine I, who legalized Christianity in the Roman Empire, summoned the First Ecumenical Council at Nicaea (AD 325), chiefly to deal with the Arian crisis. The council sought to encourage unity in the faith by further networking local Churches to help maintain that unity. It organized the Churches in a structure based on the political subdivisions of the Roman Empire. First was Rome, Church of the imperial capital and the patriarchate of the West; second was Alexandria (and all Africa); third, Antioch (and all "the East"); and by way of honor, Jerusalem and Palestine (the "dwelling place of God").

The pattern this council established would be amended by the Fourth Ecumenical Council (Chalcedon, AD 451) in a way that remained normative for centuries. There, the second place after the Old Rome was given to the New Rome (Constantinople), site of the new imperial capital. All local Churches in the empire were dependent upon these five local Churches, known as the *pentarchy*.

Eastern Christians consider each of these Churches "Apostolic Sees," connected with one or another of the first disciples of Christ. Tradition identifies Saint Peter first with Antioch and later with Rome, and depicts Saint James, the

"Lord's Brother," as the first head of the Church in Jerusalem. Local traditions recognize Alexandria as the "See of Saint Mark" and associate Constantinople with Saint Andrew, who reputedly evangelized throughout Greece. Even when other patriarchates were established beyond the confines of the empire, these older Churches were always given first place according to the order established at the early councils, partly in deference to their apostolic origins.

Over the centuries these Churches would evangelize other areas and establish "daughter Churches" in their respective territories: Rome in Western Europe, Constantinople in Eastern Europe, Alexandria in central Africa, and Antioch in the Persian Empire, India, and beyond. Even when some of these Churches became self-governing with patriarchs of their own, they were still considered "daughter Churches" of the Apostolic Sees that had given birth to them.

The relations that developed between the Apostolic Sees were markedly different from those involving these other Churches. They were not daughter Churches of one another but "sister Churches," of comparable importance and responsibility within their respective territories. The seniority of "Old Rome" was always recognized in the East, but the Eastern Churches were never dependent upon Rome, as were her daughter Churches in Europe.

As the fortunes of the Eastern Empire declined, Western churchmen tended to forget the apostolic character of the other Churches of the pentarchy and dealt with them as they would with Rome's daughter Churches in Europe. This would be a growing source of friction between them, still having effects today.

5. Championing the Trinity

The fourth century AD saw the flourishing of a free Christianity throughout the empire, leaving Christians free to disagree among themselves! A major area of discussion was the relationship of the Father and the Son. The Gospels present faith in the Trinity without explaining it fully. The Orthodox proclaimed the Father and the Son to be one in essence: "The Father and I are one" (John 10:30). The Arians reasoned that Jesus' words "The Father is greater than I" (John 14:28) show that the Son is somehow subordinate to the Father.

At the First Ecumenical Council, the bishops had come to an agreement concerning the Arian controversy. They rejected Arius's understanding of Christ and proclaimed the divinity of Christ in what would become the first part of the Nicene Creed. The Second Ecumenical Council (Constantinople I) confirmed their understanding and completed the Creed, proclaiming the equality of the Holy Spirit with the Father and the Son. This faith in the Trinity "one in essence and undivided" would be accepted by all the historic Churches of East and West.

In subsequent centuries Eastern Christians would emphasize the Trinity as a model for understanding the Church and the nature of humanity. The Trinitarian controversies would especially leave their mark on the Byzantine liturgy. The Greeks would insert a mention of the Trinity into even the most ancient of prayers. To this day the phrase "Father, Son, and Holy Spirit" is mentioned upward of twenty times in every Byzantine Divine Liturgy. Along with the Armenians, the Greeks hold their thumb and first two fingers together when making the sign of the cross as a wordless profession of faith in the Trinity. The Nicene Creed is prescribed at every Eastern Divine Liturgy.

6. "Is Christ Divided?"

While the Churches achieved unanimity in their faith in the Trinity, they reached an impasse when considering the incarnation. The fifth century saw the division of these Churches into three camps, depending on their explanation of just how Christ could be both God and man.

Like his predecessor Saint John Chrysostom, Nestorius, a Greek monk of Antioch, was chosen Archbishop of Constantinople. Nestorius found that some in the capital were calling the Virgin Mary "Mother of God" *(Theotokos)*, while others were calling her "mother of man." Nestorius proposed calling her "Mother of Christ" instead, to emphasize the distinction between the Lord's divinity and humanity.

Nestorius's position was rejected by the Third Ecumenical Council, the Council of Ephesus, in 431. Because Christianity was by now the official religion of the Roman Empire, its imperial power stood behind the conciliar decree. Nestorius's supporters fled the empire for its longstanding enemy, Persia, where they became influential in the Church of the East, which had declared itself autonomous in 424 to distance itself from Persia's enemy, Constantinople. Communication between this Church and the Churches of the empire ceased, and for many years the Church of the East came to be known as "Nestorian." Isolated from the other Churches to the West, it turned eastward, establishing missions in central and eastern Asia and developing connections with the Thomas Christians of India.

The opposite position was espoused by Cyril of Alexandria and, in particular, his successor Dioscoros. They stressed the unity of Christ's divinity and humanity, calling it "one nature" *(mia physis,* from which we get the term *Monophysite).* As the controversy developed, the Alexandrians found themselves opposed, not only by the Nestorians, but also by the Churches of the West, Rome and Constantinople. The Council of Chalcedon (451) chose a middle ground, proclaiming Christ as "one person in two natures, human and divine." Imperial power deposed Patriarch Dioscoros and replaced him with a Byzantine supporter of Chalcedon. The Monophysites countered by electing a rival patriarch, Timothy. This marks the beginning of what is known today as the Coptic Orthodox Church.

In the sixth century, the Copts were joined by some Syrians from the Patriarchate of Antioch and by the Armenian Church. These three communities, which rejected the Council of Chalcedon, would form the nucleus of what we call the Oriental Orthodox Churches. Thus by the end of the sixth century the historic Churches were divided into *Chalcedonian* (Rome, Constantinople, Jerusalem, along with the Greeks of Alexandria and Antioch), *non-Chalcedonian* (the Copts of Alexandria, the Syrians of Antioch, and the Armenians), as well as the *Nestorians* (the Church of the East). These divisions exist to this day.

While the Byzantine liturgy reflects a Trinitarian emphasis, the worship of the Syrian and Armenian Churches points toward their Christological history. Thus the "Trisagion," ascribed to the Trinity in the Byzantine Churches, is a prayer to Christ in the Syrian Churches, which often add seasonal interpolations such as "Holy God, holy mighty One, holy immortal One / You who were crucified for us / have mercy on us."

Today the historic Churches involved in these Christological controversies have begun the process of coming together again. The West, which itself has emphasized Christ's humanity, has drawn closer to the Church of the East in our lifetime. In 1994 John Paul II, Bishop of Rome and Patriarch of the West,[1] and Dinkha IV, Patriarch-Catholicos of the Church of the East, issued a common Christological declaration that acknowledged the suitability of calling the Holy Virgin both Mother of Christ and Mother of God. They added:

Whatever our Christological differences have been, we experience ourselves united today in the confession of the same faith in the Son of God who became man so that we might become children of God by his grace. We wish from now on to witness together to this faith in the One who is the Way, the Truth and the Life, proclaiming it in appropriate ways to our contemporaries so that the world may believe in the Gospel of salvation.[2]

Comparable agreements have been signed by Pope John Paul II and the heads of the Oriental Orthodox Churches. The agreement with Syrian Orthodox Patriarch of Antioch, Mar Ignatius Zakka I, says in part:

The confusions and schisms that occurred between their Churches in the later centuries, they realize today, in no way affect or touch the substance of their faith since these arose only because of differences in terminology and culture, and in the various formulae adopted by different theological schools to express the same matter. Accordingly, we find today no real basis for the sad divisions and schisms that subsequently arose between us concerning the doctrine of the Incarnation. In words and life we confess the true doctrine concerning Christ our Lord, notwithstanding the differences in interpretation of such a doctrine which arose at the time of the Council of Chalcedon.[3]

The Catholic Church also maintains an official dialogue with the Oriental Orthodox Churches as a family. At the same time, the Eastern Orthodox and Oriental Orthodox Churches, both inclined to a higher Christology, signed an agreement on their common Christological faith in 1989. Today these communities, divided since the sixth century, are calling themselves "the two families of the Orthodox Church."

7. *"People of the Book"*

The sixth through the tenth centuries have been called Western Europe's "Dark Ages." Although its political significance declined, Rome remained the first See in the pentarchy. Constantinople's importance increased through the first millennium but the three "Oriental Sees"— Alexandria, Antioch, and Jerusalem—already divided over the Council of Chalcedon, would find themselves under Arab Islamic rule by AD 641.

The new Islamic state was theocratic and therefore non-Muslims could not be citizens. "People of a Book" (that is, Jews and Christians who had received a revelation) were considered "protected" by the state, but were not members of it. The Arabs divided the Christians into separate "nations"—Nestorians, Jacobites (non-Chalcedonians), and Melkites (Chalcedonians)—each governed by its own laws, with its patriarch as the head of the nation. The development of this system resembled in many ways the creation of Indian reservations in nineteenth-century America.

Under Islamic rule, Christians were frequently restricted in their religious expression and were totally dependent on preserving the goodwill of their Muslim neighbors. As in present-day countries like Kuwait or Saudi Arabia, Christians were forbidden to "offend the believers" by ringing church bells, conducting processions or other religious observances outside the walls of their churches, or ornamenting the outside of their churches with religious symbols.[4]

Merging the Christians' religious identity with their ethnic identity served to preserve the separate identity and tradition of each group. This system also effectively ended any impetus to mission activity by these Churches until the modern era. The Ethiopian Church developed autonomously, although it retained a loose connection with its Coptic mother Church. Over the next millennium, both the Syriac Patriarchate of Antioch and the Assyrian Church of the East would see their missions eclipsed by the spread of Islam in Asia.

8. *The Emergence of the Maronites*

As we have seen, the Patriarchate of Antioch had been divided in the sixth century into Chalcedonian and non-Chalcedonian Churches. The non-Chalcedonians or Jacobites were drawn from the Syriac-speaking population, while the Chalcedonians were largely drawn from the Greek-speaking. One important exception was the Maronites: Syriac-speaking Chalcedonians, connected with the Monastery of Saint Maron in eastern Syria.

In 687 the Maronites appointed their own patriarch in the person of Saint John Maron, who had been Bishop of Batroun since 676. Some suggest that the Maronites had adopted monotheletism, the doctrine that Christ had but one will, condemned by the Sixth Ecumenical Council as denying the fullness of the incarnation. Others propose that the Maronites had become increasingly cut off from the other Chalcedonian Churches and simply wanted an accessible leader. Still others think that the Maronites, seeing the Greek Chalcedonians come increasingly under the influence of Constantinople, were seeking to maintain their Syriac identity.

In 694, the imperial army of Justinian II sought to recapture the territory conquered by the Arabs. At the same time they also attacked the Maronites. Their monastery on the Orontes was destroyed, and five hundred monks executed. After a number of further engagements, the Maronites moved high into the mountains to ensure their survival and independence and won a decisive victory at Amioun, in Mount Lebanon. For three centuries, the Maronites were cut off from the rest of the world, blockaded within their mountains. It was only when the Crusaders swarmed into the East in 1098 that the West became aware of the Maronites' continued existence.

9. *"The Flesh of God Made Visible"*

The eighth century saw the development of another defining moment in the life of several Eastern Churches: the quarrel over icons. While some early defenders of icons saw iconoclasm as influenced by Judaism or Islam, Saint John of Damascus, who articulated the theology of icons, saw it as another Christological issue. Opponents of icons feared that icons tended to Nestorianism, because they could depict Christ's *human nature* but not his *divinity*. The supporters of icons insisted that, because of the incarnation, one could not depict Christ's humanity apart from his divinity. The controversy was in some ways a repetition of the Mother of God/Mother of Christ controversy of the fifth century.

After a century of dispute, icons were solemnly restored and publicly venerated in Constantinople, an event recalled in Byzantine Churches on the First Sunday in Lent, the Sunday of Orthodoxy. More than ever, icons became a part of the spiritual and liturgical life in the Greek and, to some extent, the Coptic Churches to such a degree that, for many people today, Eastern Christianity is equated with icons.

10. *The Conversion of the Slavs*

For most of the first millennium, the area north of the Byzantine Empire was peopled by a variety of tribal groupings: Huns, Slavs, and various Turkic tribes. Both Rome and

Constantinople had sent missionaries to these peoples with varying success. A decisive moment is the Christianization of this area by the ministry of Saints Cyril and Methodius.

Natives of Thessalonika, with its mixture of Greek and Slav residents, these brothers were first sent to the Khazars, a Turkic kingdom near the Caspian Sea. In 858 they were sent by the Patriarch of Constantinople to the Moravians, in response to the invitation of Prince Rastislav:

> Our nation is baptized and yet we have no teacher to direct and instruct us and interpret the sacred scriptures. We understand neither Greek nor Latin. Some teach us one thing and some another. Furthermore, we do not understand written characters nor their meaning. Therefore send us teachers who can make known to us the words of the scriptures and their sense.[5]

Cyril devised the Glagolitic alphabet to enable the brothers to translate the Scriptures and the liturgy into the language of the Moravians. More than fifty Slavic, Caucasian, and Siberian languages currently use Cyrillic characters, now named after their creator.

The work of Cyril and Methodius was continually denounced by Frankish missionaries and as frequently endorsed by the pope. After their deaths, their followers were forced to relocate this mission to Ochrid, in Slavic Macedonia, where missions had been active since the seventh century. The Slavonic Bible and liturgy were to facilitate the conversion of the Bulgarians, Macedonians, and other Eastern Slavs over the next few centuries. Their work, which took Byzantine Christianity beyond the Greek-language orbit of the Eastern Roman Empire, would eventually render it indigenous to cultures throughout Russian Asia as far as Alaska.

Another mission of lasting significance developed in response to the request of Vladimir, Grand Prince of Kievan Rus'. Due to the work of the early Slav believers, there had been Christians in Vladimir's principality for some time, including his own grandmother Olga. In AD 988 Vladimir, aligning his realm with the Eastern Empire, put away his pagan wives, accepted baptism from a Greek metropolitan, and married the sister of Emperor Basil II. The Christianization of Kiev soon followed, and a large number of faithful were baptized in the Dnieper River.

Byzantine Christianity would become the faith of the three peoples who trace their origins to Kievan Rus': the Ukrainians, Belorussians, and Russians. As national identities developed, separate primatial sees were established at Kiev and Moscow. Considered together, the Byzantine Churches form the largest group of Christians in the world after the worldwide Roman (Latin) Church.

B. The Second Millennium

11. *Schism in Europe: The* Filioque

By the middle of the ninth century, it had become clear that the future of Europe was integrally connected with Christianity. The Bulgar Khan Boris I (852–889), together with his closest relatives, was converted to Christianity in the palace in Pliska in 864. Soon after, the Bulgarians' mass conversion to Christianity began, but was marked by increasingly bitter rivalries between Greek and Latin missionaries. Boris used this antagonism to secure the autonomy of the Bulgarian Church. After an interlude under Frankish control, the Byzantine orientation of the Church in Bulgaria was confirmed, and it was declared an autonomous arch-bishopric.

The conflict over Bulgaria brought to the forefront the growing differences between the practices of the Greek and Latin Churches. At the height of the controversy, Photios the Great, Patriarch of Constantinople, already at odds with Rome over Bulgaria, addressed an encyclical letter to the other patriarchs denouncing certain Latin practices, including fasting on Saturdays, not beginning Lent until Ash Wednesday (two days later than in the East), not allowing priests to be married or to administer confirmation, and adding the *Filioque* to the Nicene Creed. He urged the con-voking of an ecumenical council to deal with this latter point. While lesser issues would eventually be overlooked, the issue of the *Filioque* would dominate the relationship between the Greeks and Latins until modern times.

The issue had first been raised at the beginning of the ninth century. The Church in Spain had included the phrase *Filioque* in the Creed at its sixth-century Council of Toledo, assuming—as some think—that the phrase was in the Greek original. The practice gradually spread to much of Western Europe, but not to Rome. Latin monks residing on the Mount of Olives had brought back this usage with them after a trip to the West. Alerted to this innovation by monks of the famous Monastery of Saint Saba, Patriarch Thomas of Jerusalem sent an emissary to Pope Saint Leo III asking him to forbid the for-mula. Leo resisted the pressures exerted by Charlemagne to introduce the *Filioque* into the Roman liturgy and to condemn the Greeks for "deleting" it from the Creed.

The ninth-century rift between Rome and Constantinople was formally mended at the Council of Constantinople (879–880), which reaffirmed the original text of the Creed. The Franks continued to use the *Filioque,* however, and in 1014 Pope Benedict VIII allowed its use in Rome. As no longer merely a Frankish custom but the usage of the Roman Church, it would be a major factor in the separation of the Latin and Byzantine Churches. In the famous events of 1054, the Roman legate, Cardinal Humbert, would again denounce the Greeks for "deleting" the *Filioque* from the Creed! The mutual excommunications hurled at one another by the legate and the Ecumenical Patriarch, Michael Cerularius, would only be lifted in 1964 at the meeting of Pope Paul VI and the Ecumenical Patriarch Athenagoras I. In the intervening nine hundred years, decrees and theological texts on both sides would often bitterly affirm their Church's position in exclusivist terms. Whenever in the position to do so, Greeks and Latins would impose their liturgy and discipline on the others' churches.

In 2003, after several years of dialogue, the North American Orthodox-Catholic Theological Consultation, sponsored by the Catholic and Orthodox bishops, issued an Agreed Statement, *The Filioque: A Church-Dividing Issue?* After a lengthy summary of the question, it made a series of recommendations, including the following:

> That the Catholic Church, as a consequence of the normative and irrevocable dogmatic value of the Creed of 381, use the original Greek text alone in making translations of that Creed for catechetical and liturgical use;
>
> ...that the Catholic Church, following a growing theological consensus, and in particular the statements made by Pope Paul VI, declare that the condemnation made at the Second Council of Lyons (1274) of those "who presume to deny that the Holy Spirit proceeds eternally from the Father and the Son" is no longer applicable.[6]

12. *Schism in Europe: The Papacy*

Since the ninth century, the Greeks had objected both to the concept expressed in the *Filioque* and to the fact that it had been inserted unilaterally into an ecumenical creed. Once Rome had accepted the *Filioque,* however, its partisans began to insist that the pope's agreement was all that was necessary to supplant the decisions of the first councils.

Eastern Christians have always maintained the primacy of the Bishop of Rome as the tradition of both East and West. Many Eastern Catholics feel, along with their Orthodox brethren, that the exercise of this primacy in the second millennium has been increasingly above and outside the Churches and, therefore, not in the tradition. They particularly point to events of major importance that disregarded the integrity of the Eastern Churches: papal sponsorship of the Crusades, its endorsement of European colonialism in Asia and Africa, and the "Uniate" movement in Europe and the Middle East.

In recent years Western ecumenists—including Paul VI and John Paul II—have come to agree that the particular form of primacy among the Churches exercised by the Bishops of Rome has been and remains the chief point of dispute between the Orthodox and Roman Catholic Churches, and their chief obstacle to full ecclesial communion with each other, without agreeing on *how* this dispute may be resolved. Eastern Christians point to the fact that the West has elevated its understanding of the papacy to a doctrinal level, contrary to the experiences of the East, as the chief factor in this impasse.

The primatial style of the late John Paul II is universally seen as vastly different from that of an Alexander VI (1431–1503) or Pius IX (1792–1878). In the same way, few Western Catholics today would endorse the extravagant language of Don Bosco in the nineteenth century: "The pope is

God on earth....Jesus has placed the pope above the prophets...above the forerunner..., above the angels..., Jesus has set the pope at the same level as God."[7] Yet the tendency of many Western Catholics today to equate Catholic teaching with the person and writings of the current pope rather than the Church's tradition is an embarrassment to many Eastern Catholics and a reinforcement to critics that Catholics "believe in" the pope. Western Catholics should not be surprised when Eastern Catholics are reluctant to cooperate in this kind of papocentrism.

13. Attempts at Reunion

While they were often preoccupied with the political and ecclesiastical troubles of Europe, the popes periodically turned their eyes to the East in the hope of reunifying the Greek and Latin Churches. Their attempts, conditioned by the spirit of the time, were doomed to failure, and each of them left a bitter taste in the mouths of the Greeks. There were three principal attempts in this era:

1. *The Crusades:* The impetus for the First Crusade came from Pope Urban II, who promised remission of sins to those who died reclaiming the Holy Land from the Muslim Turks and Arabs who had conquered it. Crusaders successfully retook Antioch (1098) and Jerusalem (1099) and then set about creating kingdoms and principalities for themselves there. They gradually replaced the Greek hierarchs in the Patriarchates of Antioch and Jerusalem with Latin bishops. Greek patriarchs-in-exile were elected, usually residing in Constantinople and fully under the influence of the Byzantine Church. When the Crusaders were expelled, the Greek patriarchs

were able to recover their Sees and eradicate the relics of the Latin occupation.

The Crusaders were welcomed by the Armenians of Cilicia (lesser Armenia) and by the Maronites of Mount Lebanon. Both groups embraced fellowship with the Westerners and union with Rome. The Maronites accepted many Western practices, beginning a long period of latinization. The Armenians later rejected the Latin clergy's intolerance of their non-Roman liturgical customs, and abandoned their union with Rome.

In 1204 the Fourth Crusade turned its sights on the Christian Byzantine Empire. Venice, for centuries the commercial rival of Constantinople, allying with one Byzantine political faction, achieved the conquest of the city, the overthrow of the empire, and the installation of a Latin prince as emperor while exporting much of its treasures to the West. Pope Innocent III, at first dismayed at this perversion of the Crusade, took advantage of it by installing a Latin bishop, Thomas Morosini, as patriarch, and by creating Latin Sees in Byzantine territory. The pope considered this as a "reunion" of the Churches, one that was naturally rejected once the Byzantines had regained control of their nation.

In his initial shock at the siege of Constantinople, Pope Innocent III wrote to his legate, Cardinal Peter Capuanus:

> How, indeed, is the Greek Church to be brought back into ecclesiastical union and to a devotion for the Apostolic See when she has been beset with so many afflictions and persecutions that she sees in the Latins only an example of perdition and the works of darkness, so that she now, and with reason, detests the Latins more than dogs?[8]

This perception would continue in the Greek East and be confirmed by subsequent events to such an extent that the reaction of the last Byzantine prime minister, Luke Notaras, to the imminent Turkish conquest two hundred years later would become a Greek adage: "Better the turban than the tiara," an adage still repeated to this day.

In our heterogeneous and future-oriented society we find it hard to understand why many Eastern Christians still speak bitterly of the Crusades as if they happened within living memory. We feel they should "move on." In a traditional, homogeneous society, however, people do *not* move on, particularly when their history is ten times as long as that of the United States. They incorporate their past into their present, much as in the Eucharist we are "there" at Christ's sacrifice.

In his 2001 visit to Athens, Pope John Paul II acknowledged this and asked forgiveness from the Greek Orthodox Synod of Bishops for the actions of the Western Crusaders:

> Some memories are especially painful, and some events of the distant past have left deep wounds in the minds and hearts of people to this day. I am thinking of the disastrous sack of the imperial city of Constantinople, which was for so long the bastion of Christianity in the East. It is tragic that the assailants, who had set out to secure free access for Christians to the Holy Land, turned against their own brothers in the faith. The fact that they were Latin Christians fills Catholics with deep regret. How can we fail to see here the *mysterium iniquitatis* at work in the human heart? To God alone belongs judgment, and therefore we entrust the heavy burden of the past to his endless mercy, imploring him to heal the wounds which still

cause suffering to the spirit of the Greek people. Together we must work for this healing if the Europe now emerging is to be true to its identity, which is inseparable from the Christian humanism shared by East and West.[9]

In 2004, Pope John Paul II returned relics of two great Archbishops of Constantinople, Saints Gregory the Theologian and John Chrysostom, to their contemporary successor, the ecumenical patriarch. These are but a small part of what was taken from the Byzantines at the time of the Crusades.

2. *Council of Lyons (1274):* In 1261 the Byzantine Emperor Michael VIII reoccupied Constantinople. Michael feared both the Muslims in the East and the king of Naples in the West. He sought an ally in the pope and was ready to make any religious concessions to obtain the political support of the pope and his allies.

Pope Gregory X called a council at Lyons, in part to effect reunion with the Greek Church. Michael sent only his patriarch, another bishop, and several civil officials with instructions to accept the Western propositions. They accepted papal supremacy and added the *Filioque* to the Creed. Reunion was proclaimed but never entered the consciousness of the Greek Church. The pope died on the way home, and in 1281 his successor, Pope Martin IV, a supporter of the king of Naples, broke the union by excommunicating Michael. When the king's troops, with those of Venice, invaded Epirus, the reunion was officially denounced by Michael's son and successor, Andronicus II.

3. *Council of Ferrara-Florence (1438–1445):* By the fifteenth century, the thousand-year Byzantine Empire was breathing its last. Turks from central Asia had occupied most of its territory except for the immediate area of Constantinople itself. The emperor welcomed the overture of Pope Eugene IV to attempt another reunion council in the hope of obtaining Western aid. This time there was more collaborative preparation and more representative participation of the Eastern Churches. The Greek delegation included the emperor, the patriarch, and close to seven hundred others. Among the twenty-two bishops in the delegation were representatives of the Chalcedonian Patriarchs of Alexandria, Antioch, and Jerusalem.

The primary questions discussed at this council were the procession of the Holy Spirit (the *Filioque*), papal primacy, purgatory, and divergent liturgical practices (the use of unleavened bread, or *azymes,* and the "form" of the Eucharistic prayer). Some delegates also wished to discuss the distinction in Orthodox theology between the divine "essence" and the divine "energies," but the Byzantine emperor, wanting to avoid further impediments to reunion, forbade the Greek participants to raise this issue.

There was much discussion but little agreement. The Greeks would not agree that their expression "The Spirit proceeds from the Father *through* the Son" was the equivalent of the *Filioque* and continued to argue that any addition to the Creed violated the express decrees of the first ecumenical councils. They disputed the Western understanding of papal authority as universal jurisdiction and, while accepting the concept of purification after death, refused to affirm purgatory as a place of "temporal fire," as the Western theologians insisted.

Most Latin theologians in the late scholastic period tended to elevate their own departures from the common tradition into a norm, then use it to challenge those who had simply continued to believe as they always had. As a result they insisted on defining their opinions—including the liceity of inserting the *Filioque* in the Creed—as dogmatic in the decree of union. The emperor, increasingly impatient at the discussions, finally placed the most articulate Greek theologian, Mark of Ephesus, under house arrest and began a process of intimidating the other Greek bishops to sign the decree of union. It is said that, as Pope Eugene was signing the decree, he inquired whether Mark of Ephesus had signed. When he was told that Mark had not, he exclaimed, "Then we have accomplished nothing!"

Returning to Constantinople, the delegation found that the greater part of the Church supported Mark. The military aid from the West for which the emperor hoped was not enough to stop the Turkish advances, and on May 11, 1453, Constantinople fell to their assault. The survivors, attributing the demise of the empire to its acceptance of the Latin faith, renounced the union, as did the other Byzantine Churches in Europe and the Middle East. Mark of Ephesus, who had died in 1444, was glorified as one of the "Pillars of Orthodoxy."

The Turkish menace drove others to seek Roman protection. As the Greeks were leaving the council, a group of Armenians from Constantinople and the Crimea came seeking union. The pope appointed delegates to conduct discussions with them. Encouraged by their interest, he also approached the Copts and Ethiopians, each of whom sent a delegate. The decrees of union were worked out with these groups with minimal participation and called for even more acceptance of Western practices than the union with the Greeks.

Two years later, when the council had been moved again to Rome, the Nestorian Archbishop of Edessa, in the name of his patriarch, sought union with Rome. Similarly, in 1445, as the council was ending, the Nestorian and Maronite bishops of Cyprus responded to a papal initiative and appeared seeking union. The decrees of union with these groups echoed the others, but especially stressed the teachings of the third through sixth councils on the person of Christ respectively. With the Turkish conquest, all these unions were to fade into oblivion, except for the union with the Maronites.

14. *The New World Order*

When Constantinople fell to the Turks, many Greeks escaped to the West, paving the way for the Renaissance. Those who remained were recognized as the "Roman *(Rum)* nation" and placed, along with the other Orthodox patriarchates, under the civil governance of the ecumenical patriarch. As Turkish rule was extended into the Balkans, these peoples were added to the *Rum* nation. Similarly, non-Chalcedonians throughout the empire were placed under the civil authority of the Armenian Patriarch of Constantinople. This began a period, lasting almost five hundred years, in which Christians in the Ottoman Empire were increasingly reduced to the status of a ghetto, without the resources needed to support their communities. Institutions of learning, once the hallmark of Byzantine civilization, were eradicated, and within a few generations the Greek Church found itself led by largely uneducated clergy. The Turks' insistence on ethnic separatism, however, *helped* all the Eastern Churches remain as more or less intact, if impoverished, nations. Worship became their primary activity and their theologically rich liturgical texts became their primary teachers.

The destruction of the New Rome (Constantinople) contributed to the rise in prominence of the "Third Rome," as Moscow came to be called. The Slavic Churches grew in prominence in the Orthodox world, overshadowing in wealth and influence the ancient patriarchates. The independent Orthodox Romanians, and later, the Russians would provide the only financial support to their mother Churches. Yet, there was never an attempt on their part to overturn the ancient order: the Patriarchates of Constantinople, Alexandria, Antioch, and Jerusalem retained primacy over the larger, autocephalous Churches of Europe in accordance with the canons of the early councils.

Less than fifty years after the fall of Constantinople, Columbus would begin his exploratory voyages. Less than one hundred years after the end of the Byzantine Empire, the Western Church would be fractured into a host of rival religious groups in the Reformation. Both the Age of Discovery and the Reformation would have consequences for the Christian East that would change its character forever. European expansionism and Counter-Reformation theology worked together to assure that the Church of Rome expand throughout the world with the cooperation of the Catholic kings. The new religious orders would be the principal architects of this work.

15. Colonial Expansion

The discovery of the Americas intensified the commercial rivalry between Spain and Portugal. To prevent this rivalry from impeding missionary activity, Pope Alexander VI in 1493 drew a "Line of Demarcation," dividing the newly discovered world among the explorer kingdoms. He entrusted the western region to Spain and the eastern region to Portugal. A second papal decree in 1497 placed the whole East under the *diocese* of Lisbon!

When Portuguese missionaries began activity on India's Malabar (west) coast in 1500, they found a Church that had existed for centuries, the so-called Thomas or Syrian Christians, who attribute their first settlement to the Apostle Thomas. There was certainly a well-established trade between India and the Middle East in the first century, and early Christian documents from Syria locate Thomas in Persia and India. By the fourth century, the already established Malabar Church was in communication with both the Patriarchate of Antioch and the Church of the East. By the fifth century, the Thomas Christians had come under the authority of the Church of the East's metropolitan of Rewardashir, at the eastern side of the Persian Gulf.

In 1551 the Church of the East split into two groups, one of which entered into communion with Rome. Pope Julius III (1553) recognized the jurisdiction of their Patriarch Sulaqa over "All India." In 1567 Patriarch Abdiso, at the order of Pope Pius IV, assigned the See of Angamaly to a certain Mar Abraham, who enlisted the help of the Jesuits. Nonetheless, the Portuguese Archbishop of Goa, the colonial capital, refused to recognize the faith or the rites of the Thomas Christians. In 1599 he summoned them to the Synod of Diamper, condemned the (Catholic) patriarch as a heretic, forced the latinization of the Thomas Christians' rituals, and subjected them to the Portuguese Latin hierarchy and the Inquisition for India. The control of the Portuguese hierarchy—often at odds with Rome—waned at the end of the eighteenth century, but the Malabar Catholics were not given their own indigenous bishops again until 1896.

After the Synod of Diamper, the leading cleric among the Thomas Christians was the archdeacon, who served both as their civil head and the temporal administrator of the Church. He appealed for help to the Syriac Orthodox Patriarch, who sent a bishop in 1653. A rumor circulated that the Portuguese had arrested this bishop, tied him up, and cast him into the ocean. As a result, as many as twenty-five thousand Syrian Christians assembled at the open-air "Koonan Cross" in Mattancherry and swore allegiance to the throne of Antioch. They also pledged that they and their future generations would fight against the atrocities of the Roman Catholics.

The Thomas Christians were thus divided into two groups: the Malabar Catholics, following a heavily latinized form of the rites of the Church of the East, and the Syrian Orthodox Church, following the west Syrian liturgy of the Antiochian patriarchate. These groups would redivide and realign themselves often over succeeding centuries. Thus, the west Syrian tradition is today represented in India by the Syro-Malankara Catholic and by the Malankara Syrian Orthodox Churches. The east Syrian tradition is represented by the Church of the East and by the Syro-Malabar Catholics. The Mar Thoma Church broke away from the Syrian Orthodox in the nineteenth century under the influence of the Anglican mission. They follow a modified Antiochian liturgy and Reformation theology. Each of these groups has jurisdictions in North America.

The scars of this era are still affecting the Thomas Christians. In the wake of Vatican II, Rome called for a liturgical renewal in the Syro-Malabar Church, drawing them back to their Syrian roots. This provoked a crisis in the Church between those heeding this summons and those who favored the latinized rites of the past four hundred years. The community was so polarized by this controversy that Rome would not allow it to select its own bishops until 2003. Both tendencies are still found in the Syro-Malabar Church today.

Similar Church takeovers were attempted in Ethiopia in the sixteenth and seventeenth centuries. At the request of the

Portuguese king, Rome appointed a succession of Jesuits as patriarchs of Ethiopia in the hope of converting the local Church. As soon as union was proclaimed in 1626, the Jesuits began aggressively latinizing the Ethiopian Church. After ten years the Jesuits were expelled, the union abrogated, and the country closed to the Catholic Church for two hundred years.

16. *The Uniate Movement*

After wholesale attempts at reconciliation with or absorption of entire Churches at the Crusades and the reunion councils, Rome began to promote union with individuals or groups within the various Eastern Churches. Western religious, trained in Counter-Reformation apologetics, became active among Eastern Christians. Welcomed at first and often invited to preach and hear confessions in Eastern churches, they increasingly promoted the Western principles from the Council of Florence (*Filioque,* papal primacy, purgatory, and so on). In time they attracted adherents who would become the nucleus of separate Eastern Catholic Churches. Decried as proselytism or "sheep-stealing" today, this activity was perfectly consistent with the doctrine proclaimed by Eugene IV at the Council of Florence that

> all those who are outside the Catholic Church, not only pagans but also Jews or heretics and schismatics, cannot share in eternal life and will go into the everlasting fire which was prepared for the devil and his angels, unless they are joined to the Catholic Church before the end of their lives; that the unity of the ecclesiastical body is of such importance that only for those who abide in it do the Church's sacraments contribute to salvation and do fasts, almsgiving and other works of piety

and practices of the Christian militia produce eternal rewards; and that nobody can be saved, no matter how much he has given away in alms and even if he has shed his blood in the name of Christ, unless he has persevered in the bosom and the unity of the Catholic Church.[10]

This activity bore fruit due to a number of nontheological reasons as well, such as:

- *Sociopolitical status:* In Europe the traditional principle that the ruler determines the religion of the state meant that the Orthodox were disadvantaged in Roman Catholic countries and vice versa. This was an important factor in the unions of the Ukrainian Greek Catholics under Polish-Lithuanian rule (1596), and the Serbo-Croatians (1611), the Ruthenians (1646 and 1664), and the Romanians (1698, 1713) under Austro-Hungarian rule.
- *Perceived interference by higher authorities:* Resistance to the ecumenical patriarch's attempts at clerical reform contributed to the Ukrainian union in the sixteenth century, while rejection of his interference in the election of the Patriarch of Antioch played a role in the Melkite union in the eighteenth century. Similarly, Bulgarians approached Rome in 1861 in a large part to escape the restrictions on their Slavonic liturgy imposed by the Greeks. The Syro-Malankarese union of 1930 was partially due to their aversion to factionalism among the hierarchs of their own Orthodox Church.
- *Competing patriarchs:* The rejection by one part of the Church to the election of a patriarch and his replacement by another contributed to unions of the

Chaldean (1553), Syriac (1662, 1782), and Melkite Catholics (1724).

- *Individual conversions* of hierarchs or clergy prompted further missionary activity and led to the creation of a jurisdiction by Rome, as with the Armenian (1742), Coptic (1741), Ethiopian (1961), Greek (1911), and Russian Catholics (1917).

This activity naturally polarized the communities involved and led to years, if not centuries, of mutual recriminations. Often because of the involvement of civil power, there were martyrs on both sides. Thus, Ukrainian Greek Catholics revere Saint Josaphat of Polotsk, slain by anti-Polish extremists in 1623, while Ukrainian Orthodox venerate Saint Athanasius of Brest, executed by Poles in 1648. Sadly, it would take the Soviet persecutions of the twentieth century to bring members of both Churches together in suffering and in remembering those who had suffered.

The concept of Uniatism—the absorption of communities from one Church into another—was finally repudiated in 1993 with the "Balamand Statement" of the International Orthodox-Catholic Theological Dialogue. The statement decried both the proselytism, which led to the formation of the Eastern Catholic Churches, and the type of "union" to which these Churches have been subjected:

Because of the way in which Catholics and Orthodox once again consider each other in relationship to the mystery of the Church and discover each other once again as Sister Churches, this form of "missionary apostolate" described above, and which has been called "uniatism," can no longer be accepted either as a method to be followed nor as a model of the unity our Churches are seeking.

In fact, especially since the Pan-Orthodox Conferences and the Second Vatican Council, the rediscovery and the giving again of proper value to the Church as communion, both on the part of Orthodox and of Catholics, has radically altered perspectives and thus attitudes. On each side it is recognized that what Christ has entrusted to His Church—profession of apostolic faith, participation in the same sacraments, above all the one priesthood celebrating the one sacrifice of Christ, the apostolic succession of bishops—cannot be considered the exclusive property of one of our Churches. In this context it is clear that rebaptism must be avoided.

It is in this perspective that the Catholic Churches and the Orthodox Churches recognize each other as Sister Churches, responsible together for maintaining the Church of God in fidelity to the divine purpose, most especially in what concerns unity. According to the words of Pope John Paul II, the ecumenical endeavor of the Sister Churches of East and West, grounded in dialogue and prayer, is the search for perfect and total communion which is neither absorption nor fusion but a meeting in truth and love (cf. *Slavorum Apostoli*, n. 27).[11]

At the same time, the statement recognizes the right to exist of the Eastern Catholic Churches that came into being in this way and endorses their participation in the dialogue in progress between their mother Churches in the East and the Western Church. This last point is still contested, particularly in Eastern Europe, where the revival of Eastern Catholic Churches after decades of Soviet persecution is a

living rebuke to the collaborationist hierarchs who had proclaimed their "return" to Orthodoxy.

17. The Latinizing Years

Whatever their motives for requesting union with
Rome, Eastern hierarchs seeking communion generally
emphasized their fidelity to the Tradition and insisted on
respect for their legitimate practices. Thus, Metropolitan
Michael of Kiev and his bishops asked

> that we should not be compelled to any other creed,
> but that we should remain with that which was
> handed down to us...that the divine worship and
> all prayers and services of orthros, vespers, and the
> night services shall remain intact (without any
> change at all) for us according to the ancient cus-
> tom of the Eastern Church...that we should not be
> compelled to take part in processions on the day of
> Corpus Christi—that we should not have to make
> such processions with our Mysteries, inasmuch as
> our use of the Mysteries is different....[12]

Nevertheless, the misguided zeal of many Eastern Catholics,
frequently seconded by the Western religious orders working
among them, strove to create differences to further distance
their communities from the Churches from which they had
come and identify them with the Latin Church.

The earliest examples of this latinization of the Eastern
Churches were liturgical. Thus the Maronites began adopting
Western bishop's regalia and church furnishings at the time of
the Crusades. The use of unleavened bread was promoted
and the sign of the cross in the Western manner introduced.
In the thirteenth century, Western legates began insisting that
the Maronites follow Roman sacramental practices such as

confirmation by a bishop following the Roman text and the abolition of infant communion. With the development of Western-style seminaries in the sixteenth century—often directed by Western religious—this latinizing impetus accelerated. The late sixteenth century saw the Maronite patriarch issue a Romanized text of the Eucharistic liturgy, inserting the words of institution from the Roman Missal and mutilating the *epiclesis,* the prayer invoking the descent of the Holy Spirit on the bread and wine. There was a strong drive to conform Eastern sacramental rites to scholastic modalities, often by wholesale translation of the Roman ritual into Eastern languages. In addition, by the seventeenth century the Maronites had introduced the Gregorian Calendar and many Western devotions, such as the Litanies to the Blessed Virgin, into their church life.

In Europe, the insertion of the *Filioque* in the Creed and other latinizations were strongly promoted by Polish Roman Catholic clergy, in opposition to the position expressed in the Ukrainian Articles of Union cited previously. Consequently, at a 1720 synod in Zamosc, Poland, the Greek Catholic hierarchs accepted many Western practices, including the commemoration of the pope as "universal pontiff" and the addition of the *Filioque*. Many Greek Catholics in Ukraine resisted this "Polonization," as they called it, by inserting into the Creed the word *istynno* ("truly") in place of *I Syna* ("and the Son"). While many non-Byzantine Eastern Catholics accept this addition even now, Armenian and Greek Catholics have never adopted it, or have since removed it.

Major sources of latinization among all Eastern Catholics, in addition to the Western missionaries, were the Eastern seminaries and religious communities created solely on Counter-Reformation Western models. Formed in the spirit of contemporary Western religious orders, communities such as the Basilians in Europe and the Salvatorians in the

Middle East often were at odds with the hierarchy in their desire to make their Church "more truly Catholic" (that is, Latin) by imitating the practices of the West. They made various liturgical changes, such as eliminating from the liturgy the *zeon* (hot water added to the chalice before Communion) or deleting the *epiclesis,* which even Rome rejected. They introduced Western rites like Eucharistic benediction and the stations of the cross and also made disciplinary changes, relaxing marriage and fasting laws so as to induce a following among those seeking easier observances.

Western religious worked for many years to remove certain saints from Eastern liturgical calendars: John Maron (for being a Monothelite), John the Faster (for adopting the title "ecumenical patriarch"), and Gregory Palamas (for his antischolastic theology). They also promoted mandatory clerical celibacy, which several of the smaller Eastern Catholic Churches adopted in imitation of the West.

By the eighteenth century, direct latinization of Eastern liturgical practices was being discouraged by Rome, which had come to see the Eastern Catholics as "bridges" for the reconciliation of all Easterners. At the same time, another latinizing tendency was greatly encouraged by Pope Benedict XIV, who in 1752 enunciated the principle of the "preeminence" of the Latin rite: "Since the Latin rite is the rite of the holy Roman Church and this Church is mother and teacher of the other Churches, the Latin rite should be preferred to all other rites."[13] Therefore, he reasoned, Westerners should not go over to an Eastern Church. This principle also encouraged a sense of superiority among Western Catholics in Eastern regions and was cited to help draw more upwardly mobile Easterners into the Latin Church. Easterners, accepting the pope's faulty premise, developed a sense of inferiority concerning the traditions of their own Church, which would grow through the eighteenth and nineteenth centuries.

Promoted by Roman legates, the latinization of most aspects of Eastern canonical discipline, adoption of Western feasts and saints into Eastern liturgical cycles, along with the promotion of newer Western devotions, such as the Sacred Heart of Jesus and the Immaculate Heart of Mary, would increase unchecked.

While liturgical latinization had reached its peak in the eighteenth century, canonical latinization would increase in the twentieth. The nineteenth century had seen increasing unification in Europe as small principalities were merged to form kingdoms and empires. At the same time, the codification of civil laws was seen as another step away from rule at the whim of princes. In the Church, these events as well as the centralizing spirit of the First Vatican Council (Vatican I), led to the 1917 codification of Roman canon law. This law eliminated, for all practical purposes, the power of provincial or primatial structures in the West in favor of Roman centralization.

In 1927 the young Congregation for the Oriental Churches proposed to Pope Pius XI a codification for canon law for Eastern Catholics. The commission of cardinals he appointed, however, sought to submit the Eastern Catholic Churches to the Latin code. The pope rejected this idea, on the grounds that it could be interpreted as a latinization. The commission then set out to create an Eastern code, but with the Latin code as its model! Father Ivan Žužek, canonist at the Oriental Institute, would later describe this plan:

> This was the first and, in my opinion, the chief blow to the ancient Oriental Holy Canons. They were not taken as the basis for a truly oriental codification, as would have been natural. They served only to modify the Latin Code as to make it "truly Oriental." The pope's wish to remove

every vestige of latinization was gravely compromised from the very outset.[14]

The Eastern practice, on the other hand, would not be to simply replace old canons with new ones, but to compile the ancient canons and provide guidelines for implementation. In the East, the canons stemming from ecumenical councils or the pen of Church Fathers are considered elements of Holy Tradition, not to be changed by successive hierarchs. Local synods or bishops have the freedom to apply them strictly or leniently as circumstances may dictate, but not to remove them from the tradition.

Second, a common canon law for Churches as diverse in tradition as the Ethiopian Copts and the Russian Byzantines had never existed, since the various Eastern Churches follow different historical disciplines. The commission chose to "easternize" the Latin Code based almost exclusively on Byzantine sources, ignoring the traditions of the other Eastern Churches. As a result this Code has been called "apparently Byzantine, but really Latin in spirit."[15]

The "Eastern" code, the first part of which was promulgated by Pius XII in 1949, was little more than a simple repetition of most of the Western code, with a few nods toward Eastern terminology. The fourth section, published in 1957, roused the ire of many hierarchs when it in effect made the rank of patriarch equivalent to a Roman archbishop. It galvanized the bishops of the Melkite patriarchate to protest and would fuel their determination to make a forceful stand for the traditions of the East at the upcoming Second Vatican Council. Three-fifths of the code was published before the project was suspended by Pope John XXIII in 1959.

A second attempt at an Eastern code was begun in 1972 and promulgated in 1990.[16] One of the first principles set forth in the project was that all Catholics, Eastern and

Western, would follow the same procedural norms. This meant in effect that Easterners would follow the Western norms and that the Eastern code would be organized according to the categories of the Western code. Therefore, while the code was described as being drawn on Eastern sources, its canons are similar to and in some cases identical with canons in the Western code. Matters left to the particular law of the various Eastern Churches concern such things as length of terms for church offices, honorary titles, and the liturgical calendar. Thus current curial practice is loathe to admit any real autonomy to those Churches that its documents call autonomous (*sui juris*).

18. Recovery of an Eastern Identity

Paradoxically, it was the pontificate of Pius IX ("Pio Nono") that also began to turn the tide of liturgical latinization in the Eastern Catholic Churches. While Pius himself had thundered, "Nothing other is intended by the deceptive pretext of purifying rites and restoring them to their original condition than the preparation of pitfalls for the faith...,"[17] the ultra-Romanist character of his papacy and in particular his humiliating treatment of the Chaldean and Melkite patriarchs at Vatican I generated a certain sympathy for the East. His successor, Leo XIII, invited the Eastern Catholic patriarchs to Rome for consultation and incorporated many of their objections to the proselytizing activity of Western clergy and religious among their people in his encyclical *Orientalium Dignitas* (1894). Leo expressed his belief that the multiplicity of traditions did not diminish the catholicity of the Church, as some believed, but rather was the most "breathtakingly effective"[18] witness to it.

While some Westerners shared Leo's view, others thought the contrary, and local Churches suffered the consequences. A case in point was the Ethiopian Church, whose early history was noted previously. In 1849 the first Catholic bishop for Abyssinia, the Neapolitan Giustino De Jacobis, was appointed. With papal encouragement, he and his first two successors observed the local rites as much as possible. The fourth bishop took a very different approach. "According to me, who have studied the Orient with such attention," Bishop (later Cardinal) Guglielmo Massaia wrote, "the variety [of rites] is not an adornment...but an impediment to the church."[19] He insisted on observing the "pure Latin rite," a decision that was approved by the Congregation for the Propagation of the Faith in 1895. The succeeding controversy between the local clergy and their European hierarchy would only be resolved with the establishment of a separate congregation for the Oriental Churches (1917). The subsequent foundation of the Ethiopian College in Rome (1919) guaranteed the preservation of an indigenous Ethiopian Catholic Church.

Perhaps the most important step in the West's changing appreciation of Eastern Christianity was the establishment of the Pontifical Oriental Institute in 1917 by Pope Benedict XV. Where previous study of the Christian East in Rome was to refute its "heresies," the Oriental Institute became a center for a positive Catholic study of the Eastern Churches. The work of professors like Irenée Hausherr in spirituality, Tomas Spidlik in theology, Juan Mateos and Robert Taft in liturgy has revolutionized the perception of Eastern Christianity in the eyes of Westerners and among Eastern Christians as well. The present ecumenical patriarch, Bartholomew I, received his doctorate from the institute in 1968.

Isolated twentieth-century Eastern Catholic voices like Father Cyril Korolevsky (Charon) stimulated Greek Catholics first in the Middle East, then in Eastern Europe, to take a fresh look at the situation of their Churches. In Europe, Metropolitan Andriy Sheptytsky took the first steps at delatinization, under Koralevsky's influence. A similar movement, known as the "School of Cairo," led by Father Oreste Kerame, did the same in the Middle East. Their work would bear enormous fruit for the whole Catholic world at Vatican II.

The council itself would speak clearly and definitively against latinization. In its Decree on the Eastern Catholic Churches, it called for a return to the original traditions of the Eastern Churches:

> It solemnly declares that the Churches of the East, as much as those of the West, have a full right and are in duty bound to rule themselves, each in accordance with its own established disciplines, since all these are praiseworthy by reason of their venerable antiquity, more harmonious with the character of their faithful and more suited to the promotion of the good of souls.
>
> All members of the Eastern Rite should know and be convinced that they can and should always preserve their legitimate liturgical rite and their established way of life, and that these may not be altered except to obtain for themselves an organic improvement. All these, then, must be observed by the members of the Eastern rites themselves. Besides, they should attain to an ever greater knowledge and a more exact use of them, and, if in their regard they have fallen short owing to contingencies of times and persons, they should take steps to return to their ancestral traditions.[20]

In the years that followed, most Eastern Catholic Churches began to delatinize their liturgical rites. In some cases, such as the Maronite and Syro-Malabar Churches, this process was radical, because their liturgies had been the most thoroughly latinized. Today, for example, the Maronite Church has restored the unity of baptism and chrismation. It has also translated into modern languages a wealth of liturgical texts heretofore available only in Syriac. At the same time, some Eastern Catholics have adopted modern latinizations with no connections to their historic traditions, such as offering the liturgy facing the people.

Perhaps the most significant sign of the progress of delatinization among Eastern Catholics is the Profession of Faith adopted by the overwhelming majority of Melkite Greek Catholic bishops at their 1995 synod:

1. I believe everything which Eastern Orthodoxy teaches;
2. I am in communion with the Bishop of Rome as the first among the bishops, according to the limits recognized by the Holy Fathers of the East during the first millennium, before the separation.[21]

In adopting the priorities of the first millennium for the faith and practice of their Church, the bishops were proposing to all Catholics that they reexamine their own Church life and judge whether its main concerns are those of the undivided Church.

19. In the Crucible

What has been called the "Ruritanian world of European monarchs" came to an end in the twentieth century. Their passing marked a time of special trial for Eastern Christians: an era in which more of their numbers accepted martyrdom than in the three hundred years of Roman persecution before Constantine.

Life was often difficult for Christians in the Ottoman Empire, particularly for the Armenian and Assyrian/ Chaldean minorities, who were still relatively homogeneous groups living in their ancient homelands. The "Young Turks" movement—an attempt by Turkish aristocrats to modernize the Ottoman Empire in view of possible confrontations with Europe—had engineered one attempt at exterminating these minorities in 1895. Twenty years later, while Europe was distracted by World War I, they attempted to complete the work.

Accusing the Armenians of stockpiling arms and munitions for a secessionist movement, the Turkish government began eliminating them on April 24, 1915. Hundreds of the estimated 2.5 million Armenians living in the Ottoman Empire were rounded up. Upward of 1.5 million were killed or forcibly converted to Islam; many Armenian girls and women from seven to forty years of age were sold at auction. Only a minority escaped, many to the West.

Commenting on the affair, Enver Pasha, one of the ruling triumvirate, publicly declared on May 19, 1916, "The Ottoman Empire should be cleaned up of the Armenians and the Lebanese. We have destroyed the former by the sword, we shall destroy the latter through starvation."[22] Only the end of World War I and the dismantling of the empire prevented the fulfillment of this plan. In 2005 the European Union required Turkey to identify this ethnic cleansing as a genocide before Turkey could be considered for admission to the union.

The zeal of the Young Turks would be surpassed by their contemporaries, the Communists. The fall of the tsarist regime in Russia was soon followed by the first of several antireligious campaigns in the Soviet Union. Some 600 bishops, 40,000 priests, and 120,000 monks and nuns were killed during the Stalinist period alone (1922–1953), among them the Russian Greek Catholic exarchs, the Blessed New-Martyrs Leonid Feoderov and Clement Sheptytsky.

By 1922 all but the western section of Ukraine had been incorporated into the Soviet Union. The Soviet regime dedicated itself to smothering any sign of Ukrainian nationalism. They suppressed the Ukrainian and Belorussian Autocephalous Orthodox Churches in the 1920s. In the next decade they created an artificial famine by increasing the grain procurement quota for Ukraine by 44 percent to break the spirit of the Ukrainian farmer-peasants and to force them into collectivization. At the same time as the famine (1932–1934) a wave of persecutions of thousands of Ukrainian intellectuals, writers, and leaders took place to destroy Ukrainian aspirations for independence. It is estimated that roughly 18.8 percent of the Ukrainian population (some 5–8 million people) died as a result.

In 1939, the Soviets annexed western Ukraine from Poland. In 1945, as soon as World War II was over, all the Ukrainian Greek Catholic bishops were arrested or killed, union with Rome declared abolished, properties were confiscated by the state, and the Church incorporated into the Moscow Patriarchate. Similar measures were taken in Romania and Czechoslovakia. These Churches continued to function underground until the waning of Soviet power allowed them to function publicly.

The rapid revival of the Greek Catholic Church in these formerly Communist countries has surprised observers and been a source of consternation to the Orthodox Churches. These jurisdictions had willingly absorbed the Greek Catholic Churches, seeing this as a reversal of the Uniatism of previous centuries. Hit particularly hard was the Moscow Patriarchate. By the early 1950s, more than half of the Orthodox churches and monasteries in the Soviet Union were located in Ukraine, many of them Greek Catholic in origin. The end of the Soviet Union saw the revival of not only the Greek Catholic Church in Ukraine but also the autonomous Ukrainian Orthodox Churches.

This breakup of the Moscow Patriarchate in Ukraine and Roman Catholic activity in Russia itself have focused the attention of the Orthodox Churches on the Eastern Catholic Churches as the greatest obstacle to the reunion of East and West. Seeking to placate Moscow, Rome has blocked the aspirations of the Ukrainian Church to have its primate declared Patriarch of Kyiv and the desire of Russian Greek Catholics for the appointment of a bishop to their vacant exarchate. In a compromise move, Rome recently placed all Greek Catholics in Russia under the jurisdiction of a single Roman Catholic bishop, affording them a measure of canonical recognition. They thereby avoided the need for separate civil registration, which could have been opposed by the Moscow Patriarchate.

Events in the Middle East in the past fifty years—the Israeli-Palestinian conflicts, the Lebanese civil war, and the Iraqi wars—have had their effects on Eastern Christians of all Churches. Second-class citizens at best and often blamed for the interference of the presumedly Christian West, many have emigrated to Australia, Western Europe, and the Americas, weakening the Christian presence in the Holy Land for years to come.

The twentieth century's legacy of repression and violence in the Christian East has scarred the hearts of today's Eastern Christians. Nevertheless, the spirit of Christ, the victor over sin and death, has inspired some church leaders to overcome these tragedies by mutual love. As Catholics and Orthodox began contending over properties in the post-Soviet years, the Greek Catholic Patriarch of Antioch, Maximos V, and his Greek Orthodox counterpart, Ignatius IV, issued this common appeal to their Russian and Ukrainian brethren:

The experience of friendliness and reciprocal love that exists between us, the faithful of the Orthodox and Catholic Churches in our countries of the Arab East, brings us to affirm that Christian faith must be directed towards unity and not to division. From our lived experiences in the spirit of peace, in an atmosphere of understanding between the Churches and cooperative work, we invite you to transform your divisions and your troubles by surpassing them with a charitable dialogue based on our common baptism in the same Christ and in the reception of the same Spirit, by whom we became children of the same and unique Father.[23]

As of this writing, the Eastern Churches are *still* in the crucible. While the countries of the former Soviet Union are still politically unsettled, the challenges to Christian unity and mutual respect will continue. While the Middle East remains unstable, the witness of the Eastern Churches there will continue to diminish. And while Eastern Catholics are not accorded their proper autonomy and equality with the Latin Church throughout the world, the West will be ill prepared to consider union with the rest of the Christian East, autonomous since the first century.

Notes

1. On the 2006 abolition of the title Patriarch of the West, see below, page 155.

2. *Common Christological Declaration between the Catholic Church and the Assyrian Church of the East* (Vatican City, 1994), ¶5.

3. *Common Declaration of Pope John Paul II and His Holiness Mar Ignatius Zakka I Iwas* (Vatican City, 1984), no. 3.

4. See Bat Ye'or, *The Decline of Eastern Christianity under Islam: From Jihad to Dhimmitude* (Madison, Teaneck, NJ: Fairleigh Dickenson University Press and London: Associated University Presses, 1996).

5. Nestor, *The Russian Primary Chronicle*, trans. Samuel Hazzard Cross; Olgerd P. Sherbowitz-Wetzor (Cambridge, MA: Mediaeval Academy of America, 1953), 63–64.

6. *The Filioque: A Church-Dividing Issue?* An Agreed Statement of the North American Orthodox-Catholic Theological Consultation (Washington, DC, 2003), IV.

7. Saint John Bosco, *Meditazioni*, Vol. I, Ed. 2a, 89–90, cited in Maximos IV, "The Unilateral Aspect of Roman Ecclesiology," Intervention of December 5, 1962, in *L'Eglise Grecque Melkite au Councile* (Beirut: Dar al-Kalima, 1967), chap. 4.

8. Ep 136, *Patrologia Latina* 215, 669–702, trans. James Brundage, *The Crusades: A Documentary History* (Milwaukee, WI: Marquette University Press, 1962), 208–9.

9. *Address of John Paul II to His Beatitude Archbishop Christodoulos and the Bishops of the Orthodox Church of Greece* (Vatican City, 2001), 2.

10. "Decree of Union with the Copts," 1442, ¶14, in *Concilium Florentinum: Documenta et scriptores,* ed. Pontifical Oriental Institute (Rome, 1940).

11. Joint International Commission for the Theological Dialogue between the Roman Catholic Church and the Orthodox Church, "Uniatism, Method of Union of the Past, and the Present Search for Full Communion," nos. 12, 13, 14, in *Eastern Churches Journal* 1, no. 1 (1993), 17–27.

12. "Thirty-Three Articles Concerning Union with the Roman Church," no. 7 (1595), posted on *Internet Modern History Sourcebook* © Paul Halsall (source unattributed).

13. Benedict XIV, Constitution *Etsi Pastoralis* (1742), no. 2, and Encyclical Letter "To Missionaries Assigned to the Orient," *Allatae Sunt* (1755), no. 20.

14. Ivan Žužek, "The Ancient Oriental Sources of Canon Law and the Modern Legislation for Oriental Catholics," *Kanon* 1

(1973), 148, cited in John Faris, "Codification and Revision of Eastern Canon Law," *Studia Canonica,* 453.

15. Žužek, "Oriental Sources of Canon Law," 150.

16. *Code of Canons of the Eastern Churches,* Latin-English (Washington, DC: Canon Law Society of America, 1992).

17. Pius IX, Encyclical "To the Ruthenian Archbishops," *Omnem Sollicitudinem* (Rome, 1874), no. 11.

18. Leo XIII, Encyclical "On the Churches of the East," *Orientalium Dignitas* (Rome, 1894), ¶5.

19. P. Metodio Da Nembro, OFM Cap., *La Missione dei Minore Capuccini in Eritrea* (Rome, 1953), 371, cited in Fr. Kevin O'Mahoney, "The Ethiopian (Ge'ez) Catholic Rite: 1840–1979" *African Ecclesial Review* (February 1980).

20. Second Vatican Council, Decree on the Eastern Catholic Churches, *Orientalium Ecclesiarum* (Vatican City, 1965), nos. 5, 6.

21. Cited in Elias Zoghby, *We Are All Schismatics,* trans. Philip Khairallah (Newton, MA: Educational Services), 7.

22. Vahakn N. Dadrian, "Documentation of the Armenian Genocide in Turkish Sources," in Israel W. Charny, ed., *Genocide: A Critical Bibliographic Review,* Vol. 2 (London: Mansell; New York; Facts on File, 1991), 86–138.

23. Ignatius Dick, *Melkites: Greek Orthodox and Greek Catholics of the Patriarchates of Antioch, Alexandria and Jerusalem* (Roslindale, MA: Sophia Press, 2004), 121.

Chapter 2

SOME CHARACTERISTICS OF THE EASTERN CHURCHES

ASPECTS OF HOLY TRADITION IN THE CHRISTIAN EAST

A few years ago I was in conversation with the pastor of a neighboring Roman Catholic parish. We began speaking about the distinguishing characteristics of our respective traditions. My neighbor insisted that as Catholics we shared the same chief qualities that set us apart from other Christians: the Eucharist and the pope. As Easterners, after all, we were simply a different "rite" of the one Catholic Church.

Churches, Traditions, and Rites

As might be expected, my neighbor was using the "one Church" language mentioned in the preface. In this perspective, there is one Church with many "rites." This terminology, common before Vatican II, certainly does *not* express the Eastern vision of a communion of Churches. Even from a Western outlook, this terminology has come to be seen as inadequate. It identifies entire communities only from the perspective of their *liturgical* usages, and a Church is much more than that. Thus, the Vatican Congregation for the

Eastern Catholic Churches set forth a policy in 1996 that seems new but in reality reflects the older tradition:

> Certainly the tendency to reduce the specific heritage of the Eastern Churches to just its liturgical dimension should not be encouraged....The practice of the Eastern liturgy, without its entire heritage flowing into it, as into its highest expression, would risk reducing it to pure superficiality.[1]

Eastern and Western Churches certainly *do* have distinct liturgical rites, but they also have characteristic theologies, spiritualities, disciplines, and customs to distinguish them, in addition to their identity as particular Churches within a communion of faith. It is, therefore, more accurate to speak of the Maronites or Ruthenians as *Churches* of a particular *spiritual tradition* observing a distinctive *liturgical rite* within one or another *communion* (Catholic, Eastern Orthodox, or Oriental Orthodox). When we say, "Church," we speak of the community as Body of Christ. When we speak of a "tradition," we refer to the patristic heritage that forms each Church. When we say, "rite," we are talking about the liturgical usage followed by that Church. Table 1 may be helpful in illustrating these distinctions in the communion of Catholic Churches.

Table 1. Traditions and Rites of Catholic Churches

Church	Spiritual Tradition	Liturgical Rite
Armenian	Armenian	Armenian
Chaldean	Syriac	East Syrian (Edessa)
Coptic	Alexandrian	Coptic

Some Characteristics of the Eastern Churches

Church	Spiritual Tradition	Liturgical Rite
Ethiopian	Alexandrian	Ethiopian
Italo-Albanian	Greek	Byzantine
Maronite	Syriac	Elements of both Antiochian and Edessan usages
Melkite	Greek	Byzantine
Roman	Latin	Roman
Romanian	Greek	Byzantine
Russian	Greek	Byzantine
Ruthenian	Greek	Byzantine
Syriac	Syriac	West Syrian (Antioch)
Syro-Malabar	Syriac	East Syrian (Edessa)
Syro-Malankar	Syriac	West Syrian (Antioch)
Ukrainian	Greek	Byzantine

Thus, in the United States, there are ten dioceses belonging to four particular Catholic Churches (Melkite, Romanian, Ruthenian, and Ukrainian) that follow the tradition of the Greek Fathers and employ the Byzantine rite. There are seven dioceses belonging to five particular Catholic Churches (Chaldean, Maronite, Syriac, Syro-Malabar, and Syro-Malankar) following the tradition of the Syriac Fathers and employing East or West Syrian rites. There is also an Armenian Catholic eparchy with the distinctive Armenian rite and scattered Coptic and Ethiopian parishes with their Alexandrian heritage. The largest Eastern Catholic Churches in the United States are those that follow the Byzantine and Syriac traditions. While these traditions have much in common, particularly in contrast with the West, there are differences among them as well.

What Is "the Tradition"?

The most basic characteristic of any Eastern Church is the understanding that Holy Tradition is nothing less than the fruit of the Holy Spirit's presence in the Church. It is not to be confused with precedence, that is, the simple fact that something was written or taught in the past. Instead, the Eastern Churches stress tradition as a coherent stream connecting our faith and practice with that of the early Christians. The elements of the tradition—the Scriptures, the Fathers, the liturgy, and the rest—reflect the Church's living experience of the Spirit. Holy Tradition is an organic and unified stream, because the Spirit working in the Church today is the same Spirit who worked in the days of the apostles.

The core of Holy Tradition is universal: the gospel message, the Church's sacramental life, Trinitarian baptism, and the like are central to the faith and practice of every historic Church. Other elements are the proper usages of one or another particular Church, such as the type of bread used in the Eucharist. Unleavened bread points to Christ as the New Passover; leavened bread speaks of him as risen and alive. Such usages reflect an inherent diversity, because they are the expression of the Spirit working among different peoples and in different places and times. Besides these there are, of course, human habits of understanding and practice that are often called "traditions" in ordinary speech. These may support true tradition but may also empty it of meaning. Thus, it is one thing to promote parish financial support as a sign of commitment to the Church; it is quite another to make it a condition for receiving a sacrament! It is abuses like this that Christ condemned as "the traditions of men" (Mark 7:8).

Eastern Christians see their concern for Holy Tradition as of prime importance because it affirms their fidelity to the work of the Holy Spirit in the Church from the beginning. As a result, Easterners have a generally unified expression of Christian life. Theological thought and liturgical experience have not been separated, as in the medieval West. Eastern theology never came to be based on one or another philosophical system, but remained inseparably intertwined with the Church's life of prayer and worship. There is a similar unity between the liturgy of the Church and the devotional life of its people. There is no opposition between "official" worship and popular devotion. The liturgy and personal prayer reflect the same inherent unity of expression as the Church's iconography and hymnography.

The spiritual priorities of the Eastern Churches, if we can speak in such terms, reflect the insights, perspectives, and priorities of their Fathers. Their Scriptural commentaries, catechetical homilies, and manuals of Church order from the first few centuries provide pastoral models that have stood the test of time. Their theological writings, often later reworked as liturgical compositions, provided frameworks for understanding what often appears in Scripture in imagery and allusion. The Church sees this vision as evidence of the ongoing presence of the Holy Spirit within it, providing it with a continual stream of living water coming from the Fountain of life. Thus, the various Byzantine Catholic and Eastern Orthodox Churches follow the tradition of the Greek Fathers, while Churches of the Syriac tradition look to the heritage of the Syriac Fathers, and so on. While the Western Church has often throughout the course of history focused its thought and based its life on later aspects of the Church's experience, the Eastern Churches have returned again and again to the priorities of the Fathers.

Eastern Catholics formed in this way are more likely to emphasize the fidelity of current Church teaching to the tradition than the person of the teacher (the "Magisterium"). At the same time they pray regularly that their hierarchs are "rightly explaining the word of truth"[2] for the benefit of the Church.

"That They May Be One"

A second characteristic of the Catholic Eastern Churches is what we might call a commitment to communion. A local Church, with its bishop, clergy, and faithful, has access to the fullness of the life in Christ through the holy mysteries. Yet, since no Eastern Church has a monopoly on the divine life, it seeks to maintain communion with other local Churches. When the Catholic Eastern Churches came into being, it was generally those who were most open to communion with the West who joined them. By and large, these Churches maintained this communion in the face of political or ecclesiastical pressures and often at the expense of the freedom to practice their proper tradition.

In the centuries after Florence and the Counter-Reformation, this impulse to communion was based on the conviction that union with Rome was essential to salvation. Today we see that all Churches, including Rome, are bound to promote Christian unity if they wish to have the "mind of Christ." It is not a coincidence that the principal agencies of the modern ecumenical movement came into being in response to calls from the Christian East. In 1920 the Holy Synod of the Ecumenical Patriarchate issued an encyclical, "Unto All the Churches of Christ Wheresoever They Be," urging closer cooperation between separated Christian bodies. This encyclical is credited as leading to the establishment of the World Council of Churches in 1948. Similarly, it was the intervention of the Melkite Greek Catholic Patriarch Maximos IV in 1962 that led to the establishment of a permanent Secretariat for the Promotion of Christian Unity in the Catholic Church.

A consequence of this desire for communion has been the insistence on the part of many Eastern Catholics that everything possible be done to emphasize their common heritage with their non-Catholic counterparts. This has led to cooperation on both international and local levels. The regular "Fraternal Encounters" between the Ukrainian Catholic and Orthodox hierarchs of the United States and Canada, for example, has led to common position statements, observances, and the development of interparish encounters in their respective jurisdictions.

Forms of the Tradition

"In the Church God has placed apostles, prophets, teachers and every other means through which the Spirit works."[3] Thus Holy Tradition, the work of the Holy Spirit in the Church, has been expressed in many outward forms.

Each of them reflects the gospel in a different dimension, yet speaks with a common voice. Over the centuries the Church has accepted some individual examples of each of the following categories as reflecting Holy Tradition and rejected others. The foremost of these are:

Holy Scripture

While the West spoke in the Middle Ages of "Scripture *and* Tradition" (later rejected by the Reformers with their principle, "Scripture alone"), the East has generally seen the Scripture as the primary example of Holy Tradition. Later aspects of the tradition are largely based on Scripture. Liturgical prayers, for example, are often compilations of Scriptural texts strung together.

The Eastern Churches generally employ the ancient translations of the Old Testament—such as the Greek Septuagint (LXX) and the Syriac Peshitta—rather than the Hebrew text on which modern translations are based. Variant readings in the Septuagint are often quoted in the New Testament, reflecting its use in the apostolic Church. Some variants from the modern Hebrew version have been found in the Dead Sea Scrolls as well. There are English translations of both these versions available today.

In addition to the books found in Catholic Bibles, the Eastern Churches include in the Old Testament canon several books from the Septuagint: 1 Esdras and the Prayer of Manasseh (found in some editions of the Revised Standard Version and the New English Bible) as well as Psalm 151 and 3 Maccabees (also found in some editions of the Revised Standard Version). The Coptic and Ethiopian Churches employ 1 Enoch, which is considered apocryphal elsewhere.

Popular attitudes to the Scripture among Eastern Christians may be very different. I recall how the cantor in one parish I served—who had been close to the Church since his youth in Syria—approached me with a shocked expression on his face. A Protestant neighbor, discussing a biblical concept, had shown the cantor a verse in his Bible. The cantor was appalled at what he saw: the man had written in the margin and highlighted the sacred text in different colors. To the evangelical this was Bible study; to the Eastern Christian it was a desecration.

Eastern Christians approach the Scripture with a markedly unmodern sense of reverence. The Bible as the Word of God is in itself sacramental. In the Byzantine tradition, one does not even bless a Bible as one would a cross or an icon. In the home, the Scripture would be kept in the Icon Corner; in church, the Gospels would be elaborately bound and enshrined at the *bema* (in Syriac churches) or on the holy table (in Byzantine practice). A person would likely study the Bible by memorizing it—particularly the Gospels and the Psalms—and reading excerpts or digests of patristic commentaries.

Fathers of the Church

East and West revere the Fathers as our spiritual ancestors: a kind of "second generation" in Holy Tradition. While no Father is considered infallible in himself, many Fathers have come to be seen as significant catalysts in articulating the Church's teachings. Not *all* ancient writers are Fathers— many, such as Origen or Tertullian, are *not* considered Fathers. Only those whose works have been recognized as in continuity with the apostolic faith are acknowledged as vehicles of the Spirit. Unlike the West, which generally sees the age of the Fathers closed by the eighth century, the Eastern Churches set no such limits. One of the Byzantine Churches' most revered Fathers, Saint Simeon the New Theologian, died in 1022. He and Saint Gregory Nazianzen are the only Fathers to share the title "Theologian" with Saint John the Evangelist because of their immediate experience of God. Another widely revered Father in the Byzantine world is the fourteenth-century Archbishop of Thessalonika, Saint Gregory Palamas. Both Simeon and Gregory championed the possibility of personal experience of God in every age.

Besides the dogmatic Fathers, who were generally hierarchs or other clergy, the Churches also recognize ascetic masters, most of whom were *lay* monastics, men and women. Their ascetical teachings form the basis of the spiritual tradition of the Christian East. Stories from the monastic tradition still touch people seeking to live a fuller Christian life.

Church Councils

The great Trinitarian and Christological councils of the first millennium expressed the mysteries of the Trinity and the incarnation in a systematic way and established the fundamental ordering of Church structure and discipline for successive ages. These gatherings could often be contentious affairs, as Saint Gregory the Theologian witnessed: "Synods and councils I salute from a distance, for I know how troublesome they are...."[4] Yet the historic Churches have revered them as milestones in the expression of the Church's faith.

As mentioned in Chapter 1, the historic Churches continue to disagree on which councils should be called ecumenical; only Nicaea I and Constantinople I, with the Creed they produced, are accepted by *all* the historic Churches. Nevertheless these Churches are united in the Trinitarian and Christological faith that the seven formative councils of the first millennium tried to express. Byzantine Churches celebrate these councils liturgically, commemorating them on several Sundays of the year.

Based itself on a Syrian baptismal creed, the Nicene Creed came to be universally used in the Christian East. It is called the "Symbol of Faith," meaning the collecting or bringing together of the principal tenets of Christian belief. The Apostles' Creed, the most widely used statement of faith in the West, is not used in the liturgies of the Eastern Churches. It entered the Western Divine Office only between the seventh and ninth centuries.

Liturgy

All the historic Churches share a common liturgical experience. The sacramental life, built around the greater mysteries of baptism and the Eucharist, the daily offices (morning, evening, and the rest), weekly and yearly cycles of readings, feasts and fasts, and services of praise or blessing are the focus of each Church's liturgical life. At the same time, each Church has its own texts for these services with a wealth of dogmatic and poetic expressions reflecting the traditions of its own particular genius and the writings of its Fathers.

In the East the liturgical assembly became the place to experience the teachings of the Fathers. Often liturgical poetry composed by hymnographers like Saint Ephrem the Syrian and Saint Romanos the Melodist has been incorporated into the Church's worship. Doctrinal or spiritual texts by Fathers like Saint Gregory the Theologian were later recast by poets in the form of hymns.

The development of printing contributed to the standardization of liturgical texts and practices in the East as well as in the West. While the Latin Church tended to simplify and unify its texts, the Eastern Churches are more likely to collect more and more variants in their liturgical books, while excerpting from them in practice. Each Church has its own calendar of observances and cycle of readings. The principal feasts and fasts are common to most Eastern Churches but lesser commemorations are more likely to reflect the history of each particular Church.

Iconography

Icons (also *ikons*) are most common in the Byzantine, Coptic, and Ethiopian Churches. They are not as frequently used in the Armenian and Syriac Churches. They are not found in the Assyro-Chaldean tradition, where a more common image is an ornamental inscription of the divine name, *Yahwa*.

Western Christians, not accustomed to an art form that has been "canonized," are often surprised to learn that icons are not simply ornamental or devotional art. They are a truly liturgical art: venerated in liturgical services, carried in processions, and—in the Byzantine Churches—arranged in churches in a particular way that makes the church building itself an icon of the Body of Christ.

Icons are painted in prescribed ways, according to canons that indicate the models or patterns used in the composition of every subject. The process of "writing an icon," as it is called, begins with the iconographer praying and fasting. The completed icon is blessed in a liturgical service before it is offered for veneration.

The canons for the designs of icons are often, as are icons themselves, theological statements. The pattern for the icon of Christ's resurrection, often called "the harrowing of Hades," is actually a visualization of the principal hymn in the Easter liturgy. Other icon patterns have been declared uncanonical because they violate certain principles of faith. Thus, familiar Western images such as an old man as a representation of God the Father, a lamb as an image of Christ, or the dove as an image of the Holy Spirit (except in icons of Christ's baptism) are contrary to iconographic principles because the Father was not incarnate and neither the Son nor the Spirit became an animal. Icons are witnesses to the Church's faith.

Popularly, icons are not looked at as "art" but as windows to heaven, places of encounter with the kingdom of God. Recently, however, the art world has discovered the drawing power of icons and mounted sometimes elaborate exhibitions in galleries and museums. A few years ago I took a group of parishioners to such an icon exhibit in a nearby museum. As we entered the gallery, people scattered to view the many icons on display. Suddenly I heard the security guard shout, "Stop! You can't do that!" One of the parishioners had kissed an icon in veneration. "But we have to," was her reply. There is only one possible response when encountering the holy.

Witness of the Saints

It has been said that the "icons" of the Holy Spirit are the saints who lived the life in Christ in remarkable ways. Through them we see the grace of the Holy Spirit incarnate, as it were. The acts of the early martyrs, the adages of the desert ascetics, and the contemporary accounts of Spirit-filled lives continue to inspire their descendants in the faith.

The Eastern Churches look to the saints as embodying the Beatitudes and their stories as illustrations of the Church's faith in action. Stories of some early saints were actually written by Fathers of the Church. Thus, Saint Athanasius's life of Saint Anthony or Saint John Chrysostom's homilies on the martyr-saints Babylas and Ignatius of Antioch are especially revered as the witness of one saint to another.

Noted aspects of the saints' witness are often incorporated into the liturgy on days when they are remembered and their icons brought forth for special veneration. This reverence is generally in the context of the liturgy and not seen as detracting from our worship of God. We stand as one body with them before the Lord in the communion of saints and join them in glorifying him.

A Few Principles from the Tradition

The Eastern Churches return again and again to certain themes that have become central to their spirituality. Some of the principles described here are not exclusively Eastern; they are part of the patristic heritage of all the historic Churches. They may, however, receive greater emphasis in the spiritual life of one or another Eastern Church. Eastern approaches to these themes may complement or even contrast with those of the Roman Church. Neither exhausts the meaning of the gospel; this is what it means to "breathe with both lungs."[5]

The Holiness of God

One of the most distinguishing characteristics of Eastern theology is its emphasis on the utter transcendence of God. He is the Holy One, completely beyond us, and we can comprehend nothing about his essence, what (we might say) really makes him God. Yet, in a marvelous contradiction, this awesome God is totally present to us as our Father. Christ dwells in *our* midst. *We* are the temple of the Holy Spirit. The Semitic mind expresses this paradox by speaking of his name and his glory. The Greek mind uses the terms *essence* and *energies* to describe this contrast. In contrast to God's mysterious inner being (essence), his outward activity (energies) reveals himself to us. A favorite patristic illustration of this mystery was the sun: the planet itself is unapproachable, and no creature could encounter it and live. Its light, however, reaches out to us. Its heat warms us and enlivens us. Similarly, God is completely beyond us, but his Word illumines us and his Spirit gives us life.

A Scriptural expression of this thought central to Eastern spirituality is John 1:18, "No one has ever seen God; the only-begotten Son, the One who is in the bosom of the Father, he has made him known" *(translation mine)*. Traditionally, this verse is cited to prohibit the painting of an image of the Father. It is also seen as revealing the presence of the Son in the Old Testament. The words *o on*, translated as "the One," is the Greek equivalent of the divine name *Yahweh* in the Septuagint. In this thought, it is the Son, rather than the inaccessible Father, who revealed himself to Moses. This word, sometimes translated as "He who is," is a liturgical title of Christ and is placed near the head of all icons of him in the Byzantine tradition.

Vision of the Trinity

One of the most obvious characteristics of Eastern and particularly Byzantine worship is the continual reference to the Trinity, rather than to a more generic *God* or *Lord*. Practically every prayer is concluded with mention of the Trinity. The sign of the cross is made as a gesture of faith in the Trinity. The feasts of the Theophany and Pentecost are kept, not so much as historic commemorations, but as revelations of the Trinity.

The icon of the "angelic Trinity" has become the classic Byzantine image of God. Its composition suggests visions of the Trinity, the Church, and the human person that express the Fathers' theology. The three angels, drawn from the story of the hospitality of Abraham (Gen 18), sit at table, side by side, equal in rank yet distinct. The arrangement of the angels suggests a complete circle, even though no one sits at the fourth side of the table. That space is left for us, the Church, which perfects the circle. In Andrei Rublev's version of the icon, the ordinary food on the table is replaced by a single vessel, reminiscent of the Eucharist, manifesting the way we share the divine life and enter the circle. Other images of the Trinity may emphasize God's power or cosmic rule; the Byzantine icon points to the Trinity in terms of life, shared with us, in communion.

Image and Likeness

Genesis 1:26–27 depicts humanity created in the image of God and after his likeness. Modern authors generally see these terms as interchangeable, an example of the parallelism often found in the Hebrew texts. The Eastern Fathers, beginning with Saint Irenaeus in the second century, drew a distinction between them that has become fundamental in Eastern thought. The image stands for those qualities of human beings that reflect God and hint at his Trinitarian nature: conscious purposeful activity, free will, and the potential for eternal life. They saw the likeness as representing the realization of this potential, the aim of God's plan. Adam and Eve, created in God's image, were meant to grow into the likeness, and thus share in the very life of God. Sidetracked by sin, the plan would find its fulfillment only in Christ, the perfect embodiment of humanity.

In this view, every person is created in the image of God, worthy of God's love and ours. No one is so depraved that this image is completely lost. While on the one hand "there is no one who lives and does not sin" (Byzantine funeral service), there is no one created in God's image who could be thought worthless or disposable. Today, many are taught to bolster their "self-esteem" by focusing on their individual talents or assets, those things that set them apart from others. Many Eastern Christians see these attempts as misdirected. The fundamental self-worth of every human being, without exception, is their common identity in the image of God.

The image is clouded or scarred by the brokenness of humanity through sin. We may "look like" God, some have suggested, but we certainly don't *act* godlike. Yet in Christ we have the possibility of achieving likeness to God through grace.

Eastern writers also see the divine image in the communal nature of mankind. They see God's words in the Genesis story, "Let *us* make humankind in *our* image, according to *our* likeness;...male and female he created *them*" (Gen 1:26–27, italics added) as pointing to the triune essence of God as the pattern for humanity. We are created in and for relationship, as God is the loving relationship of Father, Son, and Holy Spirit.

Like mankind itself, the Church is seen in the image of the life-giving Trinity, not as a monarchy but as the "communion in the Holy Spirit" that finds its deepest realization in the Eucharist through which we are given to share in the divine life of this communion.

Theosis

That we may share in the life of the Trinity is the aim of God's plan of salvation for us. The communion intended in Paradise was frustrated by Adam's desire to "be like God" (Gen 3:5) apart from God. The Greek Fathers saw that desire as fulfilled in the incarnation of Christ: *"God became man so that man might become God."*[6] By sharing in our nature the Word sanctifies it and makes it capable once more of eternal life. In baptism we "put on Christ," receiving a share in his nature in return. Salvation, then, is not simply a matter of being saved from sin; we become "participants of the divine nature" (2 Pet 1:4) and have the Holy Spirit dwell within us.

The great icon of this "deification" or "divinization" of our humanity is the human nature of Christ, penetrated by divinity and revealed at his Transfiguration. Salvation is not simply a condition of the soul but of the whole redeemed humanity. The Church acknowledges that this final transformation awaits us "at the resurrection of the dead and the life of the age to come" (Nicene Creed) but also affirms that some saints have manifested this participation in divinity while in this life and that others have manifested it through their relics.

If the incarnation is the high point of God's plan for us, the bestowal of the Holy Spirit is its climax. "The Word became flesh in order...that we, participating in His Spirit, might be deified."[7] The Holy Spirit abides forever in the Church (see John 14:16), the "living water" promised by Christ and the source of the Church's Holy Tradition. When we approach the various elements of the Church's life in the Spirit, we can experience that life in the Spirit, which is "the pledge of our inheritance" (Eph 1:14). Confidence that Christ's promise of the Spirit has been fulfilled colors our view of Holy Tradition—Scripture, liturgy, Fathers, icons, experience of the saints—and of ministry in the Church.

Moral Thought

In the Christian East the basis for morality is not any ethical or philosophical principle but the mystery of our creation and recreation in Christ. We have been created in the image of God and therefore have within us a natural tendency toward what is good. As with everything else in us, this innate quality has been damaged by the Fall. Humanity does not automatically distinguish what is good according to God, or necessarily choose it when aware of it. We have lost that original intimacy with the One who alone can reveal to us what is true goodness and righteousness.

In Christ, however, we are called to share in the divine life. We are on the path of deification, begun in us at baptism, meant to be led by the Holy Spirit in whom we have been sealed. The Spirit's guidance is available to us in a general way through Holy Tradition and possibly in an individual way through the ministry of an elder or spiritual guide. In any case, it is our new life in Christ that is the yardstick by which we measure our actions.

The New Creation

It is not simply humanity that is renewed in Christ; *all* creation looks to be transformed in the kingdom of God.[8] The Fathers affirmed that all creation was touched by the incarnation and saw Christ's entry into the waters of the Jordan at his baptism as the sanctification of matter. We therefore bring *all* created things into our foretaste of the kingdom, blessing them and using them in our worship. Our homes, our rivers, our food all take on a richer dimension when brought into the kingdom by the prayer of the Church.

This whole dimension of our Church's life is culminated in the Divine Liturgy, our foretaste of "the Kingdom of the Father and of the Son and of the Holy Spirit." It provides a basis for the Church's commitment to praise God in paint and song, gesture and poetry, aroma and light.

The classic setting for the Divine Liturgy in the Byzantine Church is the building itself, an icon of the kingdom of God. After the iconoclastic controversy (730–842), the church building came to be filled with icons, not placed randomly or for esthetic purposes, but according to a precise order. Its purpose is to manifest visually this kingdom, which the liturgy makes present mystically. We stand before Christ the Pantocrator, surrounded by angels and saints, anticipating the time when "we will be like him, for we will see him as he is" (1 John 3:2).

Kenosis

While the Byzantine experience of worship takes us forward to the kingdom to come, its ascetic tradition points us in another direction: Christ's *emptying* of himself to take the form of a servant (see Phil 2:4–11). In public we worship the Lord of glory in the radiance of the kingdom; in secret we struggle to control our selfishness that we might imitate his service to others. Proper observance of spiritual disciplines such as fasting, rules of prayer, or obedience to an elder can make us less self-centered and more able to see Christ in those who need us to reflect God's love to them.

Eastern Christians are called to engage in a spiritual warfare in the arena of their hearts, learning to subject their brokenness to the divinizing power of the Holy Spirit working within them. Asceticism is not so much a matter of law in the Christian East as an ideal adapted to the spiritual condition of each individual, preferably with the guidance of one's confessor or elder.

"If you live alone, whose feet will you wash? Whom will you serve?" asks Saint Basil.[9] Authentic spiritual life, he suggests, demands a commitment to some form of community in our life. Christian marriage and monasticism are consecrated states of life in which believers are bound to serve one another. Service of others, however, is *not* limited to married couples or monastics, and there have never been times or places where the traditional practices of almsgiving, hospitality, and philanthropy could not be practiced.

Devoted to the tradition as they are, Eastern Christians nevertheless recognize that simply repeating the formulas of the ages apart from a relationship with God is lifeless. According to a frequently repeated adage attributed to Saint Athanasius the Great, "If you wish to live in the tradition, desire to be filled with the Spirit of God."[10] A few years ago the Greek Orthodox Archbishop Ignatius Hazim, later Patriarch Ignatius IV of Antioch, expressed the conviction common to all the Eastern Churches that the historical evidence of the Spirit's presence in the past enriches us today only when we are living the life in Christ. His words to the World Council of Churches in 1988 have often been quoted:

> Without the Holy Spirit, God is far away;
> Christ stays in the past;
> the gospel is a dead letter;
> the Church is simply an organization;
> authority, a matter of domination;
> mission, a matter of propaganda;
> the liturgy, no more than an evocation;
> Christian living, a slave morality.
> But in the Holy Spirit the cosmos is resurrected and
>   groans with the birth-pangs of the kingdom;
> the risen Christ is there;
> the gospel is the source of life;
> the Church shows forth the life of the Trinity;
> authority is a liberating service;
> mission is a Pentecost;
> the liturgy is both memorial and anticipation;
> human action is deified.[11]

Notes

1. Congregation for the Eastern Churches, *Applying the Liturgical Prescriptions of the Code of Canons of the Eastern Churches* (Rome: Libreria Editrice Vaticana, 1996), no. 13.

2. 2 Timothy 2:15, quoted in the Byzantine anaphoras of the Divine Liturgy.

3. Saint Irenaeus, *Against Heresies,* Book III, chap. 24, no. 1.

4. Saint Gregory the Theologian, Letter 124.

5. John Paul II, Apostolic Letter *Novo Millennio Ineunte* (Vatican City, 2001), no. 48.

6. Saint Athanasius the Great, *On the Incarnation,* 54.

7. Saint Athanasius the Great, *On the Decrees of the Nicene Council,* 14.

8. See Romans 8:20–23.

9. Saint Basil the Great, *Little Asceticon,* question 3.9.

10. *Introduction to Holy Tradition* (McKees Rocks, PA: God With Us Publications, 1988), 7.

11. Ignatius Hazim, Address to the World Council of Churches, cited in *With Eyes of Faith: An Introduction to Eastern Theology* (McKees Rocks, PA: God With Us Publications, 1985), 56.

Chapter 3

COMING TO AMERICA

NINETEENTH- AND TWENTIETH-
CENTURY IMMIGRATIONS
FROM THE CHRISTIAN EAST

Most families in the United States and Canada can recall stories of their immigrant "pioneers" to the New World. My own father came to the United States in 1904, an eight-year-old boy traveling alone to join his family, who had emigrated the previous year. The treasures he brought with him were a bit of money entrusted to him by relatives back home—quickly lost aboard ship—and two icons, given to preserve him in the old faith in his new land. His story typifies the nineteenth- and early twentieth-century immigrant experience. They brought little with them in the way of material possessions but much in the way of the faith of their ancestors, around which they would build their new lives.

The first immigration of Eastern Catholics to the Western Hemisphere took place from the 1870s until just after World War I. Carpathian and Ukrainian Greek Catholics, many recruited to work in the mills and mines of the Northeast (often as strikebreakers), made up the largest number. In the 1890s, agents recruiting in Eastern Europe brought a number of Ukrainians to homestead the prairie in western Canada. It is estimated that almost half of the

Greek Catholics in the Austro-Hungarian Empire had emigrated by 1920.

The second largest group consisted of Maronites, Melkite Greek Catholics, and Eastern Orthodox from Lebanon and Syria. A number had settled in the Midwest. Some had been brought to staff the Middle Eastern "village" at the 1893 Columbian Exposition; others traveled the railroads as peddlers, ultimately to become storekeepers in towns along the right-of-way. Many more worked in the textile and haberdashery of New York and New England or, in their characteristically independent way, struggled to develop their own small businesses.

The reception they were accorded and the circumstances in which they lived were similar to that of other immigrants of the period. These Eastern European and Middle Eastern immigrants usually came with no knowledge of English and a great number—up to 40 percent—were illiterate in *any* language. Cultural differences were great. The 1899 Report of the Associated Charities of Boston, describing the city's Syrian immigrants, asserted that "next to the Chinese, who can never be in any real sense American, they are the most foreign of all our foreigners."[1] What it means to be "really American" would be at the root of the Eastern Catholics' trials through much of the twentieth century.

The "Menace" of Diversity

In 1882 a group of Greek Catholic immigrants in Shenandoah, Pennsylvania, petitioned their metropolitan in Europe, Sylvester Sembratovich, Archbishop of Lviv, to send them a priest:

> We are not entirely the same as we were in our own country, because something is lacking to us. Lacking to us is God, a God Whom we could

understand, Whom we could adore in our own way. You, Your Excellency, are our father here, too, because you are the father of the Rusins. Therefore we beseech you: give us our priests, give your blessing towards the building of churches, so that in this new land we may have that which is holy in the land of Rus'.[2]

In response, the metropolitan encouraged them and sent a priest, Father Ivan Volansky, to serve his spiritual children.

On arrival, Father Volansky approached the local Polish Roman Catholic pastor to request the temporary use of his church. Refused, the Greek Catholics rented a hall and began their own parish on Saint Nicholas's Day 1884, according to the Julian calendar. Neither the priest nor the metropolitan imagined that the Greek Catholics were not free to establish their own church. As a courtesy, Father Volansky attempted to visit the local Roman Catholic hierarch, Archbishop Patrick J. Ryan of Philadelphia. Arriving at the Philadelphia chancery, Father Volansky was met by the vicar general of the archdiocese, Reverend Ignatius Horstmann, who refused to allow Volansky to exercise his priestly ministry or even see the archbishop because he was married.

The Greek Catholic tradition of a married clergy, common to most Eastern Churches, is that married men could be ordained deacons and priests, as mentioned in the Pastoral Epistles (1 Tim 3:1–13; Titus 1:5–9). Once ordained, however, a priest or deacon could *not* marry. The growing influence of monasticism during the first millennium had made clerical celibacy widespread in the West and mandated for the Western Church by the Second Lateran Council (AD 1139). Similarly in the Byzantine Church celibacy came to be required of bishops (but *only* bishops—not deacons or priests) by the Trullan Synod (AD 692). Married men elected to the episcopate were expected to separate voluntarily from their wives. Bishops have since been chosen from the monastic, celibate, or widowed clergy. There had never been any attempt to curtail this practice, as old as the Church itself, since union with Rome. The Roman Catholic bishops in the United States, however, had no experience with Eastern Catholics; the only married clergy they knew were Protestants!

The American Roman Catholic bishops had recognized the need for non-English-speaking parishes for the Germans, Italians, Poles, and others. However, they had no idea that there were Catholics who not only spoke different languages, but even used them in their liturgies, which were so strange to Westerners. The bishops could not conceive that these people belonged to different Catholic Churches. They expected all Catholics to come under their jurisdiction and observe their discipline.

The Greek Catholics, believing themselves to be under the jurisdiction of their own metropolitan in Europe, proceeded to build their own churches, rectories, and—when denied burial in Roman Catholic cemeteries—their own places of internment as well. Greek Catholic priests continued to establish parishes among their people, although considered schismatic by the Latin bishops. By 1890 there were thirty-two priests organizing Greek Catholic parishes in the United States.

In Canada, Greek Catholic priests were actually solicited by the government. An agent of the Dominion Lands and Immigration Department wrote to Ottawa as early as the summer of 1896 to send "one or two priests with the next batch of emigrants," asserting that "this is a highly important matter to the colonists and should receive early attention."[3] Again, local Roman Catholic bishops reacted strongly against these priests and the churches they established.

From the first, the Greek Catholic churches were established by the people who established lay brotherhoods for this work, similar to those they had known in Europe. Any funds they collected or property they bought were held in the name of the brotherhoods or the congregation, many times because they did not trust the local bishops. Thus, in 1910, there were ninety-three Greek Catholic churches in Canada, but only one was held in the name of a Roman Catholic diocese.

The conflict between the Greek Catholics and the Roman bishops came to a head in 1889. Father Alexis Toth[4] had come to serve the newly constructed Greek Catholic church in Minneapolis. As instructed by his bishop in Europe, Toth presented himself to Archbishop John Ireland. Toth later noted that, as soon as the archbishop realized that Father Toth was a Greek Catholic, his hands began to shake. He asked whether Toth had a wife and learned he was a widower. The archbishop summarily rejected Father Toth, saying, "I do not consider that either you or this bishop of yours are Catholic." The two argued, and Ireland publicly informed his priests that Toth was not a regularly ordained priest and was to be avoided. It is ironic that Archbishop Ireland was known as the leading "Americanist" among the hierarchy, promoting democracy as the best possible system for a pluralistic society. He also believed that the largely immigrant Catholic Church must eliminate all their foreign traits for the Church to become truly American. His efforts to standardize the Church were anything but democratic.

The Greek Catholics, smarting at the insult to their Church and clergy, were at a loss as to what to do. Father Toth later recalled, "Some of the parishioners stated, 'Let us go to the Russian bishop—why should we always bow before strangers?'"[5] He approached Russian Orthodox Bishop Vladimir of San Francisco, who received him and his parish into the Orthodox Church in 1891. Father Toth would later say, "The Roman bishop forced me to convert over to the Orthodox. I was driven to it."[6] In any event, Father Toth began canvassing the Greek Catholic parishes, persuading them to follow his lead. By 1900, thirteen Greek Catholic parishes had been accepted into Orthodoxy. Within a few years at least thirty thousand Greek Catholics had joined the Orthodox Church. Father Toth was recognized as one of the pioneers of Orthodoxy in the United States and was canonized in 1994 by the Orthodox Church in America.

The Roman Catholic hierarchy reacted by attempting to persuade Rome to curtail Greek Catholic practices in America, particularly the married clergy. It is, they said,

> a constant menace to the chastity of our unmarried clergy....The sooner this point of discipline is abolished before these evils obtain large proportions, the better for religion, because the possible loss of a few souls of the Greek Rite bears no proportion to the blessings resulting from the uniformity of discipline.[7]

The remaining Greek Catholic clergy established a committee to deal with the Roman Catholic bishops. They asked that the married clergy be permitted to function, since they had very few unmarried priests in Europe. They also asked that a Greek Catholic priest be appointed as a kind of vicar general for all their parishes. Unfamiliar with multiple jurisdictions in the more pluralistic areas of the Balkans and the Middle East, the archbishops were opposed to any kind of separate jurisdiction for the Greek Catholics in the United States. Instead, they requested that the senior archbishop, Cardinal Gibbons of Baltimore, inquire of the Vatican whether the Roman rite exclusively should be observed in the United States. The Congregation for the Propagation of the

Faith responded by affirming the acceptability of Eastern Catholic parishes in America, provided that they were subject to the local Roman Catholic bishops. The Congregation also directed that the Greek Catholic bishops not send any priests to America except through them and that only celibates or widowers were acceptable for service among the immigrants.

Most Greek Catholics refused to follow the rule of hierarchs who showed such public contempt for the tradition, as, for example, the bishop of Pittsburgh, who publicly affirmed that "a married priest could not be good or a Catholic!"[8] Priests traveled from parish to parish to avoid being restricted by the local bishop. Churches were erected and other properties purchased in the name of laypeople, and a general contempt for the episcopate resulted. Finally, in 1907, Rome acknowledged the need for a Greek Catholic bishop in America. Pope Pius X appointed Soter Ortynsky, a renowned preacher, as bishop, but in the bull *Ea Semper* imposed several restrictions on his ministry. Bishop Soter was not entrusted with full authority and had to function at the discretion of each Roman bishop. He was also charged to enforce several discriminatory restrictions desired by the American hierarchy, including clerical celibacy, celebration of chrismation by a bishop only, and separation of Eastern Catholic hierarchs in America from their mother Churches. Most Greek Catholic clergy simply refused to adjust their practices to accommodate the Latin bishops, and the people refused to turn over properties to a bishop who had no independent authority. Finally, in 1913, Bishop Soter was named exarch and given ordinary jurisdiction; the most offensive restrictions of *Ea Semper* were rescinded. Canadian Greek Catholics had been given an exarch, Bishop Nikita Budka, the previous year.

The question of married clergy—which the Vatican Secretary for the Eastern Churches, Cardinal Sincero, described as "a cause of painful perplexity or scandal to the majority of American Catholics"⁹—would be revived in 1929. A decree of Pope Pius XI forbad the service of married Greek Catholic priests in the United States, requiring them to return to Europe. A weaker Greek Catholic bishop attempted to enforce this decree, and history repeated itself as thousands of American Greek Catholics, dedicated to safeguarding the Eastern heritage of their Church, severed communion with Rome. These independent parishes soon realized their need for episcopal oversight and appealed to the ecumenical patriarch, who received them into the Orthodox Church. This jurisdiction, in time, would be known as the American Carpatho-Russian Orthodox Greek Catholic Diocese, headquartered in Johnstown, Pennsylvania.

Today, although restrictive regulations are still technically in force, married clergy serve parishes in all ten Greek Catholic eparchies in the United States without opposition from the Roman Catholic episcopate. Several married Eastern Catholic priests have been given biritual faculties and function in Roman Catholic parishes, schools, and hospitals as well as in the military. Some Latin bishops have understandably objected to Western Catholics seeking to be ordained as clergy in the Eastern Catholic Churches. Eastern Catholic hierarchs, on their part, are not interested in ordaining men who are not committed to their Churches and who are simply seeking to be married priests one way or another. Other Western bishops are interested in seeing how their Eastern counterparts face the challenges associated with married clergy in contemporary society, such as ministering to widowed clergy and the partners in failing marriages or to the needs of clergy wives who may have careers of their own.

Attempts to restrict Eastern Catholics in this matter continue in Europe. In 2001, Cardinal Keith O'Brien, Archbishop of St. Andrews and Edinburgh, publicized a

Vatican request that bishops in Western Europe raise a barrier to married Greek Catholic priests serving among new immigrants in their countries. The Italian Bishops' Conference immediately requested the Ukrainian hierarchy to avoid sending married priests to minister to their faithful in Italy, because "they would create confusion among our faithful"[10] despite the fact that the existing Greek Catholic eparchies in Italy retain their long-standing tradition of married clergy. Other European episcopates followed suit.

In a similar move, the Vatican Secretary of State, Cardinal Angelo Sodano, had directed married priests in Poland to "make a return to their homeland,"[11] that is, Ukraine, without taking into account that they were living in their homeland. What had really moved were the borders, in the redrawing of boundaries after World War II! Cardinals Achille Silvestrini of the Oriental Congregation and Edward Cassidy of the Secretariat for Promoting Christian Unity took up their defense, and Sodano canceled the order.

The contrast between the universally mandated priestly celibacy in the West and the optional married or celibate priesthood of the East became an issue as recently as the 2005 Synod of Bishops. Insisting on universal celibacy, Cardinal Angelo Scola of Venice asserted that there are "profound theological motives" for the practice, although he did not cite any. He was corrected by the Melkite Patriarch of Antioch, Gregory III, who, pointing to the tradition of married clergy in the Eastern Churches, insisted that mandatory celibacy "has no theological foundation."

Trusteeism

The first Greek Catholic parishes in America, as we have seen, were established by laypeople who then sought the services of their clergy from Europe. In this they somewhat paralleled the experience of Roman Catholics in eighteenth-century America who established parishes before there were priests to serve them. In both cases, the congregations provided and controlled the parish finances and held the property they purchased in their own name. This would raise another red flag in the eyes of post–Vatican I bishops who saw this as another instance of trusteeism or "Americanism."

The first Roman Catholic hierarch in America, John Carroll, who served from 1784 to 1815 first as apostolic prefect, then bishop, and finally Archbishop of Baltimore, had promoted ideas that were very different from the monarchist bishops of Europe. He endorsed concepts like the separation of church and state, the election of bishops by the local clergy, and the use of English in the liturgy. At the beginning of his episcopate he also supported the system of parish administration by lay trustees but changed his mind after conflict with German immigrants in Philadelphia. He had established Holy Trinity parish for them in 1788 but when they had built a church and sought to appoint their own priest, a struggle ensued that resulted in the church being placed under interdict.

There were places where the trustee system worked well. Influenced by the democratic ideals of the new nation, Bishop John England of Charleston developed a constitution for his diocese modeled on the American Constitution and organized regular diocesan conventions of clergy and laity to study the affairs of the diocese. Conflicts between the Church establishment and new immigrants, however, would determine the future of lay involvement in American Catholic parishes.

The growing mix of ethnic groups in America found expression in increased tension between independent-minded congregations of one background and more authoritarian hierarchs of another. The "second generation" of Roman

Catholic bishops in America included several French hierarchs who associated republicanism with the French Revolution—and had little use for it—and a continually increasing number of Irish bishops who knew no tradition of lay administration. New York and Philadelphia soon became centers of lay resistance to the management style of their new bishops. Trustees attempted to hire and fire pastors, even over the objection of the bishop. The First Provincial Council in the American Church (1829) came out against the system that had provoked a schism in Philadelphia in 1826, when the trustees barred the bishop from his own cathedral. The growing dominance of Irish American bishops and the antirepublican sentiment of leading European churchmen would limit the influence of trustees in most American Catholic parishes until the immigration of the 1870s and 1880s. It would be the arrival of Lithuanian, Polish, and Slovak Roman Catholics seeking their own church structures that would raise the issue of lay trusteeism again.

When Greek Catholic parishes began to split into Catholic and Orthodox factions in reaction to Roman Catholic resistance to their traditions, lay control of properties became an even more pressing issue. The decree establishing the Greek Catholic episcopate, *Ea Semper,* charged the new bishop with seeing that the Church's property and other assets were placed under episcopal control. Parishioners, priests, and bishops on both sides of the controversy went to court to lay claim to parish properties and assets. These lawsuits were often complicated by the fact that deeds and bank accounts were held locally and often did not explicitly refer to any higher Church body. The litigants themselves often did not recognize English-language descriptions of their own Church name or traditions, causing further confusion. The antagonisms generated by these lawsuits at the turn of the century often divided families and fueled animosities that would affect parish, family, and community life for fifty years. The division of the 1930s mentioned previously would add to these tensions as Catholics, "Independents," and Orthodox struggled for control of parishes. Many people, disgusted at the years of wrangling, left for Roman Catholic or Protestant churches—or no church at all.

While administration of parish properties was often in the hands of laypeople in Europe and the Middle East, there was one significant difference in America. Abroad, these committees or brotherhoods often had the recognition of the state as well as the Church. In the Ottoman Empire, for example, each recognized Church (Armenian, Greek Catholic, Orthodox, and so on) had its "higher" or "national" council made up of the leading members of the community, which managed the extensive holdings of these Churches. They were made up even then of the more prominent landowners, educators, members of parliament, and government ministers. In America, where immigrants usually came from the lower economic and educational segments of their homelands, their committees reflected their simpler origins. The result was that factionalism and strife became characteristic of Church life.

Slavic Greek Catholics had established a number of religious mutual benefit societies, which also assisted in the building of their churches. Among the Ruthenians, for example, the Greek Catholic Union, the Rusyn National Union, and the Society of Russian Brotherhood had hundreds of chapters in the United States by 1910. Today, such organizations are chiefly fraternal, and the Slavic Greek Catholic Churches, whose life was dominated for so many years by the trusteeism controversies, have little or no lay involvement in the administration of their Churches. Other Eastern Catholic communities, some made up of more recent immigrants, have the tradition of and structures for lay participation, such as diocesan conventions and pastoral councils on both eparchial and parochial levels. The challenge to these Churches is to ensure that their active laity be well grounded in the spiritual basis of Church ministry. Without this formation, parish and diocesan councils often more resemble social or ethnic clubs rather than ecclesial entities.

Nationalism and the Churches

A third important factor in the life of some Eastern Catholic Churches has been connected to the political situation in these communities' countries of origin. Much of Europe and Asia Minor experienced years of turmoil in the twentieth century. Nationalist movements at the beginning of the century engaged the hearts of many émigré clergy and laity. As soon as the first Greek Catholic bishop, a Galician, was installed in the United States, he was accused of fostering Ukrainian nationalism by many Carpathian clergy and people under his jurisdiction. The controversy became so heated that Rome divided the exarchate on the death of Bishop Soter in 1916, placing Greek Catholics from the metropolitanate of Halych in one jurisdiction and those of other eparchies in a second. These two exarchates would eventually become the eparchies of Philadelphia and Pittsburgh respectively.

World War I and its aftermath affected Eastern Christians in different ways. Canada, because of its ties to Great Britain, was in the war from the very beginning. Its War Measures Act of 1914 resulted in the internment of more than eighty-five hundred "enemy aliens," of whom more than five thousand were Ukrainians who had emigrated to Canada from territories under the control of the Austro-Hungarian Empire. An additional eighty thousand people (of whom the vast majority were Ukrainians) were obliged to register as "enemy aliens" and then required to report to local authorities on a regular basis.[12]

Far from being Austrian partisans, Ukrainian immigrants were intensely nationalistic. Many became involved in the political movements that resulted in a brief period of Ukrainian independence before the territory was ultimately divided between Poland and the Soviet Union in 1921. This nationalistic spirit would find expression in the Church. In Canada, a number of the Ukrainian intelligentsia came into conflict with the pro-Austrian Greek Catholic bishop, and led the movement to establish an autonomous Ukrainian Church, independent of any higher authority, be it Rome, Constantinople, or Moscow. The Ukrainian Union of Teachers in Canada convoked a series of meetings resulting in the establishment of the Ukrainian Greek Orthodox Church in Canada (1918) and in the United States (1920). This Church's membership would be considerably augmented by Orthodox Ukrainians fleeing the Soviet takeover of eastern Ukraine in 1921.

Nationalist sentiment was also strong among the persecuted peoples under Ottoman rule, particularly the Armenians, who would also suffer under the Soviets, and the Assyrians, whose homeland, promised self-determination by the British mandate, was ultimately divided among Iran, Iraq, Syria, and Turkey. Proponents of conflicting political viewpoints would trouble their Churches here for many years. Their churches in America, like those of the Greeks— many of whom had been expelled from Turkish territory after World War I—would also focus on preserving their national ethos and their language as expressions of their Christian identity. Churches operated after-school or Saturday school programs to pass on their language and culture to the young and developed folkloric dance and music groups, which would tour parishes and develop their ethnic

American identity. Unlike some jurisdictions, which admitted the use of English in worship with the coming of age of their second generation, these Churches would resist any attempts to replace their ancient language in the liturgy. They also discouraged their young from marrying outside of their ethnic community.

One largely Christian area of the Ottoman Empire to achieve nationhood was Lebanon, home to many Middle Eastern Christians, particularly the Maronites. The largest single religious group in the country, the Maronites wholeheartedly identified their Church with Lebanon; yet they did not feel the need to insist on Lebanese language and culture as the focus of their émigré parishes. With the promise of their own nation, some Lebanese immigrants sought to return home, but the famine and hardship resulting from World War I meant that few could sustain themselves in its precarious economy. Most remained in the West.

Nationalist sentiment would affect the organization of other Eastern Churches as well. Prior to 1917 there had been only one Orthodox jurisdiction in America, under the Patriarchate of Moscow, and embracing Orthodox of several ethnic groups. As a result of the Russian Revolution, communications between the North American Diocese and the Church in Russia were greatly hindered. In the early 1920s the Patriarch of Moscow, Saint Tikhon, who had served as Bishop of the North American diocese for ten years, called on his dioceses outside the borders of the Soviet Union to organize themselves autonomously until such time as normal communications and relations with the Russian Church could resume. Shortly thereafter, at a council of all hierarchs, clergy, and lay delegates, its diocese in the United States declared its autonomy. Concurrently, several ethnic groups, which had been an integral part of the single diocese, organized separate jurisdictions and placed themselves under their respective mother Churches. This gave rise to the present situation of Orthodoxy in North America, namely, the existence of multiple, overlapping jurisdictions based on ethnic background rather than following their canonical principle of a single Church entity in a given territory. As a result of this move to ethnic identification, non-Hellenic Orthodox and Greek Catholics began substituting terms such as "Byzantine" or "Eastern" for *Greek* in the titles of their Churches, to avoid being categorized as ethnic Greeks.

Other Churches Seeking Recognition

Enough Middle Eastern immigrants remained in North and South America that Melkite Greek Catholic and Maronite bishops were sent to the Americas in 1921–1922 to evaluate the status of their Churches here. Both Melkite Metropolitan Maximos Saigh and Maronite Bishop Chukrallah Khouri petitioned the Oriental Congregation to establish episcopates for their Churches, but nothing would be done until the era of Vatican II. The metropolitan, later Patriarch Maximos IV, would write many years later:

> In order to look after them [immigrant faithful], their priests, their works and their future we had been asking for a number of years for the establishment of a simply personal hierarchy since the Latin hierarchy, even with the best of intentions, could not effectively look after them....Thousands of reasons were found to deny us what we were requesting. We were told that the episcopate of the country refused, but when a Latin hierarchy was established in the very heart of the East, our counsel was not requested.[13]

Exarchates would be established only in 1966 for Melkites and Maronites and in 1982 for Romanian Greek Catholics.

Eastern Catholics faced other hurdles in seeking recognition of their existence and traditions. Two significant challenges took place practically on the eve of Vatican II. In 1959 Cardinal Alfredo Ottaviani, Secretary of the Holy Office (formerly the Supreme Sacred Congregation of the Roman and Universal Inquisition and now the Congregation for the Doctrine of the Faith), attempted to restrict the Eastern Catholic Churches in two ways. Greek Catholics in Israel were directed not to evangelize Jews; this was reserved to the Latin Patriarchate. Similar restrictions were attempted in the United States. Archbishop George Hakim of Nazareth (later Patriarch Maximos V) replied, "In whose name can a Catholic bishop be forbidden to preach the Word to the non-Christians in his diocese and convert them?"[14]

One month later, a similar directive was issued prohibiting the use of modern Western languages in the liturgy because it would "give the opportunity to promoters of the abandonment of Latin in the Holy Liturgy to cite them as an example and precedent."[15] While Greek and Syriac were the liturgical languages of the Melkite and Maronite Churches respectively, they had long mingled the vernacular Arabic into the celebration, particularly in Scripture readings and longer prayers. In the United States, English had been introduced around 1950 in a natural way, as English became the first language of most parishioners.

Informed of the controversy, Melkite Patriarch Maximos IV personally intervened with Pope John XXIII, "Our 'Arabic' in the United States is English; in Paris it is French; in Argentina it is Spanish, etc. Hence we are permitted to celebrate in the living language everywhere and the local hierarchy must be informed...."[16]

Both these prohibitions were largely ignored, and in the wake of Vatican II they were forgotten. English became the principal language in many Eastern churches and Westerners became members of Eastern Catholic parishes in increasing numbers. After Vatican II, the Apostolic Delegate to the United States, Archbishop Egidio Vagnozzi, would write:

> American society is in a very real sense a pluralis-tic society—religiously, culturally, politically, socially, ethnically, etc. There is room for a variety of Rites within the Church in the United States. Each of our Catholic Rites has much to offer through its own forms, its own discipline, its own style of Christian living.[17]

Archbishop Vagnozzi encouraged Eastern Catholics to pro-mote their traditions in this country, "offering this genuine Christian way of worship and life to all those who may find it a more desirable and more effective means to become closer to God and to His Church."[18]

Assimilation and the Second Generation

In 1924, the U.S. Congress passed an act to limit the immigration of aliens into the United States. The law estab-lished quotas based on the number of foreign-born residents from each country according to the 1890 census. Thus, while the annual number of immigrants allowed from the Irish republic was 28,567, the quota from Greece and the Middle Eastern countries was the minimum: 100. Since their home territories were not independent nations, no quotas were established for the Ukrainians and Ruthenians. With the exception of some Russian and Ukrainian Greek Catholics admitted as refugees from the Soviet Union, immi-gration of Eastern Catholics slowed to a trickle until the end of World War II. In Canada, the number of immigrants continued to rise. By 1931, for example, Ukrainians made up the second largest ethnic group in Winnipeg, Manitoba, accounting for 8.5 percent of the population.

In the years between the two World Wars, most Eastern Catholic communities were made up of second- and third-generation ethnic Americans. While they may have spoken their parents' language at home in deference to the "old folks," their language was English and their way of life was increasingly American. While the first immigrants were tenacious in their defense of Church traditions, many of their children barely understood them. Mary Pawlak in her self-published *Bald Mountain Childhood* epitomized the experience of this generation. "Nobody ever spoke any English in church until after Father Kraskevitch retired...," she wrote.

> The services were three hours, three hours long. They had no pews, no seats, in the church then. You had to stand the whole time. And the sermons were in Russian and they talked in a special way with their voices, so I didn't know much what they were saying. Church wasn't anything we looked forward to exactly.[19]

Aware of the gap between immigrant parents and their Americanized children, many Eastern Catholic pastors realized that, without early intervention, the next generation would be godless. Many encouraged their parishioners to send their children to Roman Catholic parochial schools for the grounding in faith and morals their parents could not communicate to them. In many cases, this strategy resulted in these families simply becoming Roman Catholics and raising their children the "American way." Eastern Catholic students in parochial schools who remained in their own

Churches were often singled out in class because they made the sign of the cross "backward" or didn't know basic Roman Catholic practices. They were regularly made to feel inferior and longed to fit in like everyone else.

In reaction, Eastern Catholic parishes often attempted to hold on to their parishioners by "Americanizing." In practice, this often meant that they adjusted the customs of their own Churches to Roman Catholic models. Anything unfamiliar to Western Christians was downplayed or eliminated. Icons were replaced with statues and stations of the cross. Bearded clergy shaved to look more American and adapted their vestments to Western patterns. Servers were dressed in cassocks and surplices instead of their proper liturgical garments. Choir members donned robes like their Methodist neighbors. Parishes replaced liturgical services like matins and vespers with Western devotions, such as novenas or the recitation of the rosary. As new churches were built, they were constructed on purely American (that is, Western) lines.

Many Eastern Catholic priests sought to distance themselves from their Orthodox counterparts or gain acceptance from Roman Catholic colleagues by adapting Western practices. By the 1930s most were being educated in Roman Catholic seminaries in America. Few studied abroad in their mother Churches. They had little formation in their own liturgical tradition, and none at all in the spirituality underlying it. They were ill equipped to catechize their parishioners in the particular ethos of their Church and saw many traditional practices as simply old-fashioned. Rev. Stephen Gulovich, a priest of the Pittsburgh Greek Catholic exarchate, was typical of this approach when he wrote:

> Enthusiasts and armchair champions of the Eastern rites often condemn efforts aimed at the

revision of the Eastern liturgies because they are not familiar with the difficulties encountered by the clergy, who must make the best of a ritual which does not fit in its entirety into the circumstances of contemporary life. They do not seem to understand that our generation no longer has the patience to sit (much less stand) through services which last for hours, such as the rather monotonous Good Friday Matins of the Byzantine rite, or the long monastic vigil service on Christmas Eve....

In a similar manner these idealists do not hesitate to condemn the American Byzantine clergy for sometimes abandoning the eikonostasis. They do not realize that the artistic and structural atrocities which often pass as eikonostases are not only unliturgical, but frequently either makes it impossible for the majority of faithful present to follow the action in the sanctuary or distracts their attention from the action altogether. These are some of the reasons why the American faithful often insist that the eikonostasis be omitted from the more modern structures.[20]

Ironically, it is precisely these elements that so many Westerners came to appreciate once they were presented in an intelligible and prayerful manner. Every year as I was growing up, forty to fifty Catholic high school students used to come every year with their teachers to attend Good Friday matins in our parish. Much of the service was in English (long before Vatican II) and the meaning of the most important prayers explained. Many of the youths returned year after year.

By the 1950s, more and more books on the Eastern Churches, liturgy, and iconography were making their appearance from both Eastern and Western sources. With the announcement of Vatican II, Western Catholics took an interest in the Eastern Churches, and Eastern liturgies were offered with increasing frequency in Roman Catholic parishes, schools, and seminaries. These movements served to awaken the interest of many Eastern Catholics as well. They saw the advisability of designing new churches on Eastern rather than Western models. They began to appreciate and employ the work of master iconographers and craftspeople to create works of liturgical art that were fully in line with liturgical tradition, not simply copies of nineteenth-century renditions. This generation increasingly accepted and took pride in its uniqueness, abandoning the Westernized practices of the previous age.

Renewed Immigration: Eastern Europe

The aftermath of World War II brought about a renewed immigration of Ukrainian Greek Catholics to the West. During the war, many Ukrainians, such as the blessed New Martyr Emilian Kovch, had opposed Nazism and died for protecting Jews. Others, however, had allied themselves with the Germans who had enlisted their aid in the "fight against Communism." With the defeat of Germany by the Allies (which included the Soviet Union), they became political refugees. After the war, the Soviet Union annexed western Ukraine (Galicia or Halych) and began the systematic destruction of the Greek Catholic Church there. This caused another massive wave of immigration. Accorded protection from religious persecution, they joined other displaced persons in emigrating to the West.

While the first Ukrainians had come to America for economic reasons, this wave came as political and religious refugees. They intensified the ethnic character of their

Church, centering their life in America on the folk music, dance, and politics of their oppressed homeland. These émigrés were not interested in Americanizing; if anything, they were dedicated to maintaining precisely the traditions of their homeland. Many had as their aim a return to Ukraine once the Soviet regime was ousted. They often found it hard to adjust to the Westernizations made in the Churches by the descendants of the first immigrants. Some were particularly devoted to observing the Julian calendar in solidarity with Ukrainians in Europe.[21] This sometimes resulted in the establishment of Julian calendar parishes in close proximity to older churches that had adopted the Gregorian calendar. Some parishes were obliged to observe both calendars for the major feasts and even for every Sunday.

One of the ways in which Ukrainians at the end of the twentieth century expressed the particular identity of their Churches, both Catholic and Orthodox, has been through the use of the Ukrainian language. While some Greek Catholics under Austrian rule had replaced Church Slavonic with the vernacular (Croatian, Hungarian, Romanian) in earlier centuries, the Ukrainians had preserved its use until the "Russian occupation" of their Church and homeland after World War II. Many also rejected as "Russian" the use of the three-bar cross, although it was actually of Greek origin. And so, while other Eastern Churches were replacing older languages with English, the Ukrainian parishes put a greater emphasis on the use of contemporary Ukrainian in worship.

Another major expression of Ukrainian identity among this group has been the support generated for recognition of a Ukrainian Greek Catholic patriarchate. Many Ukrainians, both Catholics and Orthodox, saw the Patriarchate of Moscow as allied with the rulers of the Soviet Union in the repression of Ukraine. Aided by their coreligionists in the West, a number of Ukrainian Orthodox formed their own jurisdiction, the Patriarchate of Kyiv, although most of the country's Orthodox Christians—particularly in the Russian-speaking East—are still allied with the Moscow Patriarchate.

In 1963 the Metropolitan of Lviv, Joseph Slypij, was released from a Soviet prison after eighteen years of captivity and allowed to leave for the West. The pope immediately named him "major archbishop" of the Ukrainian Greek Catholic Church. As the Greek Catholic Church developed in the West, three other metropolitanates came into being in Canada, Poland, and the United States. While, in Eastern practice, an autonomous Church may be headed by an archbishop or metropolitan (the Orthodox Church of Cyprus, of apostolic origin, and the Church of Greece are prime examples), it is not common for one metropolitan to have others under him. In such cases the normal title for the senior metropolitan would be "patriarch." The Vatican, however, invented a new designation, "major archbishop," unknown in the East, for the Ukrainian primate. The head of the Syro-Malabar Catholics, and more recently the Romanian Greek Catholic metropolitan and the Syro-Malankara Catholicos were given the same title.

Metropolitan Joseph, living in exile in Rome, became the center of the Ukrainian émigré community throughout the world, which began a drive to have him recognized as patriarch. Ukrainians throughout the world formed associations, foundations, and periodicals devoted to this cause. Their insistence on promoting this issue often set them against local bishops who commemorated Kyr Joseph as major archbishop. The Vatican, sensitive to charges of fostering Uniatism, has not recognized the Greek Catholic patriarchate; nevertheless, Ukrainian bishops throughout the world now generally commemorate their primate as patriarch.

Although the Greek Catholic Church in Ukraine had come into being when the Metropolitan of Kyiv united with

Rome in the sixteenth century, subsequent political align-
ments resulted in the Catholics being concentrated around
Lviv in western Ukraine, and the Orthodox in the eastern
and southern provinces. The Greek Catholic primate was no
longer styled "of Kyiv" but "of Lviv."

In 2001, the current patriarch, Lubomyr Husar,
declared his intention to reclaim Kyiv as his See city. In the
Soviet era there were several mass relocations of peoples,
resulting in Ukrainian Greek Catholic communities in the
east and throughout Asiatic Russia. Greek Catholics were no
longer restricted to western Ukraine but were found
throughout the country, for which ten new eparchies and
exarchates have been established since 1993. Patriarch
Lubomyr laid the cornerstone of a new patriarchal cathedral
in Kyiv in 2002, and in 2005 formally established his See in
Kyiv as the center of the Greek Catholic Church in Eastern
Europe. While this move was denounced as proselytism by
the Moscow patriarchate, it was welcomed by Ukrainian
Orthodox hierarchs who attended the patriarch's first liturgy
in Kyiv, along with a Georgian Orthodox bishop.

The breakup of the Soviet Union in 1991 also saw a
new wave of immigration from Eastern Europe. These newcomers were not political or religious refugees. Like the
immigrants of the nineteenth century, they came seeking economic advancement. Unlike their predecessors of a century
ago, they were often well-educated professionals or entre-
preneurs. Many maintained business connections with their
home countries. Because their Church had been repressed in
the Soviet era, many are dedicated believers. Unlike the
immigrants of the 1940s or 1950s, however, they are more
interested in American technology than European folklore.
Interviewed in the *New York Press,* Ukrainian journalist
Olha Kuzmowycz, age eighty-four, noted:

When I go to a concert or lectures now, I see always the same old people. You almost never see the young people coming. And this community is shrinking and shrinking. The only thing that is not shrinking now is the church, because the fourth wave, they came to the church. They go to the church, but they almost never go to lectures or concerts.[22]

Renewed Immigration: The Middle East

To a lesser degree, other displaced peoples, including many Eastern Christians from the Middle East, emigrated for political and religious reasons in the last quarter of the twentieth century. This resulted in the appearance of other Eastern Christian groups in the West for the first time. The easing of U.S. immigration laws in 1965 brought many to the United States, resulting in the establishment of new parishes, dioceses, and other ecclesiastical structures. These countries include:

- *Egypt:* For almost two hundred years the intellectual and economic leadership of Egypt had been dominated by Greeks and Syrians, brought in by Mohammed Ali Pasha, viceroy of Egypt (1769–1849), in his drive to modernize the country. In 1961, the Egyptian president Gamal Abdel Nasser nationalized all their businesses and institutions, causing most of these Greek Catholics and Orthodox to emigrate. The rise of Islamic fundamentalism in the same era prompted the first emigration of Copts to the West and the first establishment of this Church outside its ancient homeland.
- *Ethiopia and Eritrea:* In 1974, a Marxist revolution engineered by a military junta known as the *Derg*

abolished the Ethiopian monarchy and established a one-party socialist state. The Ethiopian Orthodox Church was disestablished and, in 1977, its patriarch arrested and slain along with hundreds of monks and thousands of others in a five-year "Red Terror." Several coups, drought, and subsequent famine resulted in the first large-scale emigration of Ethiopians to the West, the defeat of the *Derg* in 1991, and the secession of the province of Eritrea the next year. Further emigration resulted from border wars with Eritrea that began in 1998.

- *Iran and Iraq:* Targeted for extermination by Turkish and Kurdish troops (1915–1918), members of the Assyrian/Chaldean people were promised a homeland of their own in northern Mesopotamia by the British. By 1922 it was clear that this minority was to be sacrificed to other interests and their prospective "homeland" divided among Iraq, Syria, and Turkey. At the end of the British mandate (1933), the Assyrian/ Chaldean people were attacked by Iraqi troops. Many were slain and others, including the patriarch of the Church of the East, were deported. The patriarchs have made their home in the United States ever since. Their number in the West increased dramatically during the Iraqi war with Iran throughout most of the 1980s, when many were deported as being "of Persian ancestry." The Gulf War (1991) and the 2003 American invasion of Iraq multiplied the number of Christians fleeing Iraq, and the Chaldeans make up what is arguably the largest Eastern Catholic community in the United States today.

- *Israel and Palestine:* Another minority caught in the middle, Palestinian Christians first began emigrating to the West in 1948 when many Orthodox, Greek

Catholic, and Maronite villages were depopulated by the Israeli military. Successive wars and uprisings as well as pressures to emigrate from both Jews and Muslims have driven most Palestinian Christians to the West, emptying the Holy Land of much of its Christian population.

- *Jordan:* Expelled by the Israelis, many Palestinians went to neighboring Jordan. Forced to struggle even harder for economic survival, Jordanian Christians began emigrating to the West, where they joined existing Orthodox and Greek Catholic communities.

- *Lebanon:* Under pressure from Israelis, Palestinians, and Syrians alike, the Lebanese endured a fifteen-year-long civil war (1975–1990). Many Christians were driven from their homes and sought refuge in the West. While many returned to Lebanon at the war's end, a number remained, expanding the Lebanese Christian communities in the West.

- *India:* While not the result of political or religious oppression, the widespread immigration of Indian Christians began for the first time in the 1960s. Many of the immigrants were graduate students or professionals whose education exceeded the opportunities available to them in India. With reputedly the highest educational attainment among Asians, these Indians came seeking economic advancement appropriate to their educational backgrounds. The Syro-Malabar and Syro-Malankara Catholic communities as well as the Malankara Syrian Orthodox and Mar Thoma Churches began organizing at this time, adding still another dimension to the picture of Eastern Christianity in America.

Notes

1. Report of the Associated Charities of Boston (1899), 56, 57, cited in Jean and Kahlil Gibran, *Kahlil Gibran: His Life and Work* (New York: Interlink Publishing Group, 1981).

2. Cited in Isadore Sokhocky, "The Ukrainian Catholic Church of the Byzantine Rite," in *The Ukrainian Catholic Metropolia in the U.S.A.* (Philadelphia: Archeparchy of Philadelphia, 1959), 200.

3. Cited in John Panchuk, *First Ukrainian Church in Canada* (Winnipeg: Trident Press, 1974, in Ukrainian).

4. Keith S. Russin, "The Right Reverend Alexis G. Toth and the Religious Hybrid." Unpublished dissertation submitted to St. Vladimir's Seminary, 1971. An abridgment of this monograph was published in *St. Vladimir's Seminary Quarterly* 16, no. 3 (1972) as "Father Alexis G. Toth and the Wilkes-Barre Litigations."

5. Russin, "Toth and Religious Hybrid," 38; "Toth and Wilkes-Barre Litigations," 132.

6. Russin, "Toth and Religious Hybrid," 39. This citation was omitted in the published article.

7. Resolution of the Roman Catholic Archbishops in America (1893) cited in Robert Hospodar, *Clash of Titans: Subcarpathian Ruthenians, New Immigrants in a New Land,* 7, "A Constant Menace: the Issue of Married Priests in America." Originally serialized in *Eastern Catholic Life* (West Paterson, NJ: Eparchy of Passaic), posted on the Catholic Information Network (www.cin.org/clash).

8. Hospodar, art. cit.

9. Victor J. Popishil, "Clerical Celibacy in the Eastern Rite Catholic Dioceses of the United States and Canada," *Diakonia* 2, 2 (1967), 143.

10. Cited in Sandro Magister, "The Vatican against Immigration: Entry Denied to Priests with Wives and Children" (October 20, 2003; available at *www.chiesa.espressonline.it*).

11. Ibid.

12. See Lubomyr Luciuk, *A Time for Atonement: Canada's First National Internment Operations and the Ukrainian Canadians 1914–1920* (Kingston, Ontario: Limestone Press, 1988, in Ukrainian).

13. *L'Eglise Melkite Grecque Catholique au Concile* (Beirut: Dar al-Kalima, 1966), 313–14.

14. Maximos IV, *The Eastern Churches and Catholic Unity* (Freiburg: Herder and Edinburgh/London: Nelson, 1963), 13.

15. Letter of the Apostolic Delegate, Archbishop A. G. Cicognani, to Archbishop T. J. Toolen, cited in Joseph Tawil, *The Courage to Be Ourselves* (unpublished manuscript).

16. Synodal Observation on the First Schema on the Eastern Churches, cited in *L'Eglise*.

17. Egidio Vagnozzi, "Rites and the People of God," *Melkite Digest,* II, no. IX (November 1966), pp. 1–4.

18. Ibid., p. 4.

19. Mary Pawlak, *Bald Mountain Childhood,* posted on htpp://home.swipnet.se/roland/genealogy.html by Roland Anderson as "an autobiographic, biographic, and historical description of growing up in a Carpatho-Rusyn family on Bald Mountain near Wilkes-Barre, Pennsylvania during the 1920s and 1930s."

20. Stephen C. Gulovich, "The Ruthenian Exarchate in the United States," *Eastern Churches Quarterly,* vi (London 1946), pp. 459–485.

21. See chap. 4, pp. 106–107.

22. Roksolana Luchkan and Andrey Slivka, "Ukrainian East Village: A Shortened Oral History of an Immigrant Neighborhood," *New York Press,* 14, no. 22, 2001, pp. 22–26.

Chapter 4

THE EASTERN CATHOLIC PARISH IN AMERICA

THE EXPERIENCE OF EASTERN CATHOLICS TODAY

Attending college in New York City, I became friendly with a Roman Catholic girl who had grown up in a small Pennsylvania town. Although the town had no Roman Catholic church, there was a Greek Catholic church, which my friend attended when she couldn't get to her own parish church in the next town. Her experience was the exact opposite of most American Catholics who may live near several Roman Catholic churches but have never even seen an Eastern Catholic or an Eastern church of any kind.

Western Christians—Catholic or Protestant—who *do* have the opportunity to visit an Eastern church are often surprised by what they see and hear. A few years ago public radio commentator and convert to Orthodox Christianity Frederica Mathewes-Green authored an article, "First Visit to an Orthodox Church—Twelve Things I Wish I'd Known,"[1] in which she listed a number of things that might surprise a Western visitor, such as the Nicene Creed without the *Filioque*.

If you've read the first chapter of this book, you already know why the Byzantine Churches, Catholic or Orthodox, don't have this phrase in the Creed. Following are a number of other things you might find surprising in one or another Eastern Catholic parish.

The Church Building

The Eastern parish you visit may be located in a former home or a recycled Western church that was adapted for Eastern purposes. If the parish meets in a building specifically built in an Eastern tradition, you may notice some of the following:

- *One or more domes:* The classic rotunda became normative for Byzantine churches with the construction of Hagia Sophia, the Great Church of Constantinople, in the sixth century. Ideal in Mediterranean climates, these domes could not sustain winter snowfalls and were adapted in central and northern Europe. Armenian churches often have a conical dome, a style that came to typify their national architecture. Slavic churches often are surmounted by one or more tapered "onion" domes, so named because they look like...onions! Maronite churches may be topped by a cross with two or, more generally, three parallel crossbars. The lowest of the three bars on Slav Byzantine crosses is generally slanted. This is sometimes interpreted to refer to the criminals crucified with Christ, one of whom repented and was promised Paradise (see Luke 23:43). Chaldean churches are recognizable by massive square towers we might associate with ancient Babylon.
- *Church interiors:* After the iconoclastic controversy, Byzantine and Coptic church buildings came to be filled with icons, not placed randomly or for esthetic purposes, but according to a precise order. Their

purpose is to manifest visually the heavenly kingdom, which the liturgy makes present mystically. We
stand before Christ the Pantocrator (the most
prominent image in the church, typically in the
dome), surrounded by angels and saints, anticipating the time when "he shall come again in glory"
(Nicene Creed). Armenian churches typically have
an image over the altar of the Mother of God hold-
ing Christ. Syriac churches generally have no specific arrangement for iconography.

- *Where's the altar?* With their strong emphasis on the
unknowable essence of God, Eastern Churches have
generally maintained some form of separation
between the holy place, representative of the presence
of God, and the rest of the church. In Armenian,
Assyro-Chaldean, and Syriac churches this separation
may be in the form of a curtain, in some churches similar to a theater curtain, which is drawn aside during
much, if not all of the liturgy. In Byzantine and Coptic
churches, this separation is generally in the form of a
screen or wall, pierced by three doors and covered
with rows of icons. In addition to the lowest row of
icons of Christ, his mother, John the Baptist, and the
parish patron, the icon screen *(iconostasis)* may have
additional rows of icons featuring the Great Feasts of
the Church year, the apostles, prophets, and patriarchs. The icon screen shows that the inaccessible God
has become accessible in Christ, foretold by the
prophets, incarnate of the Virgin, proclaimed by the
apostles and the Church. In front of the curtain or
icon screen is an open area in which certain liturgical
actions are conducted. This is particularly important
in some Syriac churches as the location for the Liturgy
of the Word.

- *Church seating:* While most Eastern parish churches in America have pews or seats in at least part of the church, some may not. Even if they do, don't be surprised if some people stand through the entire service, since seating was traditionally for the elderly or infirm. Standing, kneeling, or making prostrations are the typical prayer stances in Eastern Churches. Sitting was either reserved to the bishop and his presbyterate or only considered appropriate for listening. In many Eastern Churches, the First Nicene Council's prohibition of kneeling (a penitential position) on Sundays or during Paschaltide is still observed. In any case, there is often nothing like the uniformity of posture generally found in Western congregations. Some people may stand throughout the liturgy, others may sit, or move about the church to light candles or venerate icons. In some parishes made up of more recent immigrants, particularly from Asia, men and women may be seated on different sides of the church, although this practice is changing even abroad.
- *Where's the confessional?* Confessions are usually heard in front of an icon of Christ, which may be at the front of the church or in a side room, or at the step of the sanctuary. Since absolution is conferred by the laying-on-of-hands in the Byzantine and Syriac traditions, Western confessionals are impractical, although some Eastern Catholics have adopted them.

Worshiping in an Eastern Church

Western Catholics are accustomed to bless themselves with holy water at the church door. In Byzantine churches, people usually light a candle and venerate icons of the church patron and the occurring feast, which may be placed on stands near the door or on a table at the front of the church, before going to their place. In some Syriac churches, it is the Gospel Book rather than an icon that may be displayed for veneration. Members of the Syriac churches of India generally leave their shoes at the church door before they enter the nave. In some Coptic and Syriac churches of the Middle East, those entering the sanctuary remove their shoes at that point, as Moses was told to do at the burning bush: "Come no closer! Remove the sandals from your feet, for the place on which you are standing is holy ground" (Exod 3:5).

In some Slavic churches, people may obtain a *prosphora* (altar bread) at the church door. They offer it along with a list of their prayer intentions for the priest to commemorate at the liturgy. The unused remainder of the loaf may be returned to the offerer at the end of the liturgy.

First-time visitors may wonder about the following:

- *How many times do people bless themselves?* In the Eastern Churches, the traditional gesture upon entering the church is a bow, called a *metany,* usually accompanied by the sign of the cross. In some Eastern Churches prostrations are common. These gestures are often repeated at the singing of the Trisagion ("Holy God, Holy Mighty One...") in the Byzantine and Syriac traditions. People in the Byzantine churches bless themselves whenever the Father, the Son, and the Holy Spirit are mentioned.
- *I thought I was early but they've already started!* The liturgy is often preceded by one of the daily offices such as *orthros* (matins) or the third hour. In larger parishes other services, such as the churching of a newborn child or memorial services for the departed, may regularly be held in connection with the liturgy.

In Slav Byzantine parishes, *molebens* (devotional prayer services) may also be held after the liturgy.

- *Don't they ever stop singing?* Not often. The greater part of most services in the Eastern Churches is generally sung. Some parishes, particularly those of Slavic background, have choirs; others have cantors. In both cases, the congregation may sing along, either softly (called "subsinging") or robustly. A few prayers (the Creed, the Lord's Prayer, and the Prayer before Communion) may be recited, but just about everything else will be sung. In the Byzantine tradition, musical instruments are not used, although church bells may be rung at prescribed times. In Syriac and Coptic parishes, the use of cymbals and other instruments may be prescribed at certain times in the services. Many parishes have incorporated the organ into their liturgical worship.

- *They're coming this way!* Liturgical action is not restricted to the sanctuary. In several Eastern traditions, there are processions around the church interior at every liturgy bringing the Gospel Book, the holy gifts, or icons into the congregation. Worshipers of Middle Eastern background will often reach out and touch these sacred objects or kiss the end of the priest's robe as they pass. In some Syriac churches, the Liturgy of the Word is celebrated from the *bema* or platform in front of the sanctuary. In Byzantine churches, additional services such as memorials are conducted there or at side shrines designated for that purpose. At the end of the liturgy, the priest may come forward again to offer the hand cross or Gospel for veneration, distribute blessed bread, or anoint the faithful on feast days.

In Armenian and Syriac churches, deacons and servers go down the aisles passing the Peace before the Eucharistic Prayer. In Syriac churches people pass the Peace by taking the joined hands of their neighbor between their own two hands. Armenians pass the Peace by placing their right hands over their hearts (as in the American Pledge of Allegiance), bowing over the right and then the left shoulder of their neighbor saying, "Christ is revealed amongst us." The neighbor responds, "Blessed is the revelation of Christ." In Byzantine churches, the Peace is generally only exchanged by the clergy, but the greeting may be said aloud to the people: "Christ be in our midst! He both is and ever shall be." Many Eastern Christians also use seasonal greetings in and outside the liturgy at Pascha, the feast of the Resurrection ("Christ is risen—Indeed He is risen") and at Christmas ("Christ is born—Glorify Him").

- *How should I receive Holy Communion?* The common Eastern practice is to receive in both kinds, but the methods of administration differ. In most Byzantine churches, the Lamb (Eucharistic bread) is broken and placed in the chalice, and Communion is distributed using a spoon. The communicant should open his or her mouth widely without extending the tongue so the priest can drop the Eucharist into the mouth. Other Eastern Churches administer this mystery by intinction: dipping the consecrated Bread into the cup and then placing on the tongue. Still others offer each species separately: the communicant approaches the priest for the Bread and then moves to a deacon to drink from the cup. Commonly people approach the priest with both hands folded across the chest.

- *They're eating something.* Food and drink are frequently blessed in the Eastern Churches. In Byzantine churches, festal bread (often stamped with an icon of the feast) is blessed along with wheat, wine, and oil on many feasts. On Pascha the foods from which people had fasted during the previous forty days (meat, eggs, cheese, and other dairy products) are blessed. At memorial services a sweetened wheat cereal or sweet bread may be blessed and distributed. Other festive foods include water (January 6, Feast of the Theophany) and fruit, especially grapes (August 6, Feast of the Transfiguration). At the Divine Liturgy, the unconsecrated remainder of the bread offered may be distributed after Communion or at the end of the liturgy. People eat it, then give it to others, or take it home to give absent family members a share in the celebration. In Orthodox parishes, the Eucharist is not given to non-Orthodox. However, parishioners may offer visitors a piece of this blessed bread as a gesture of hospitality.
- *It's Christmas and the church is closed!* One of the most confusing aspects of Eastern Christianity for Westerners is the Church calendar. Remember that all Christians followed the Julian calendar until Pope Gregory's revision in the sixteenth century. At the same time the pope revised the method for determining the date of Easter. Roman Catholic countries adopted these changes quickly. Protestant countries (including Britain and its American colonies) did not follow for some years. Some Eastern Christians have yet to adopt it. They still follow the Julian or Old Calendar, which is currently thirteen days behind the Gregorian Calendar. Thus, December 25 in the Julian Calendar will fall on January 7 in the Gregorian.

Many Slav Byzantine churches, Catholic as well as Orthodox, in addition to Copts and some Syriac churches follow this calendar.

Other Eastern Churches adopted the Gregorian Calendar for the fixed feasts (those that occur on the same date every year, like Christmas) but rejected Pope Gregory's method for computing Easter and the observances in the paschal cycle. Sometimes, "Greek" or "Russian" Easter falls on the same date as the Western feast, but it may be one, two, or even five weeks later. According to the computation established at the First Nicene Council in 325, Pascha should not be celebrated with the Jewish Passover. The Orthodox Churches interpreted this to mean that Pascha may not begin until after the Passover feast, accounting for the discrepancy. In the West, Antiochian, Greek, and some other Orthodox Churches follow this "mixed" calendar. While some Eastern Catholics in Europe and the Middle East observe it as well, those in the West generally follow either the Old or New Calendar consistently. All Armenian, Assyro-Chaldean, and Indian Churches follow the Gregorian Calendar for all observances.

The Sacramental Life

The Eastern Churches generally use the term *mysteries* to refer to what the West calls "sacraments." The Western term comes from a Latin word for "sign," emphasizing the external, visible rite, while the Eastern term stresses the unseen meaning of that rite for our life in Christ. All Eastern Churches employ the same holy mysteries as the West, but in different ways and with slightly different rites:

- *Baptism* is normally performed by triple immersion in water, highlighting Saint Paul's image of baptism as union in the death and resurrection of Christ (Rom 6:5–8). Since baptism in water and the Spirit are one (John 3:5), baptism is immediately sealed by the gift of the Holy Spirit in...
- *Chrismation* at whatever age the candidate may be. Once initiated into the life in Christ, the new Christian may call upon God as Father and share in the Lord's Eucharistic table. In the latinizing period after the Council of Trent, some of the Eastern Catholic Churches were drawn to the Western practice of separating Baptism and Chrismation (Confirmation) and/or withholding the Eucharist until the age of discretion. Today, Baptism and Chrismation are given together again in most Eastern Catholic Churches. In the Byzantine Churches these mysteries are followed once more by the...
- *Eucharist:* The newly baptized may simply be communicated from the reserved Gifts, or the christening service may be joined to the Divine Liturgy. Other Eastern Catholics currently follow the Western custom of First Communion at the age of reason.
- *Repentance:* The practice of frequent private confession to a priest was not, at first, common in the Eastern Churches, which saw this mystery as a "second baptism," reuniting penitents to the Church after serious sin. Reception of the Eucharist, given "for the forgiveness of sins" (Byzantine liturgy), with a repentant heart would remit "daily sins." Private confession, practiced especially during the fasting seasons of the Church year and on the occasion of pilgrimages or retreats, later became common in most Eastern Churches. In the Byzantine and Syriac traditions, the

priest says the absolution prayer while placing his stole on the head of the penitent. Some Eastern Catholics, such as the Armenians and Chaldeans, adopted the Western form for confession in its entirety. In many Byzantine churches, private confession is given in the context of a penitential service.

Some Churches made confession a required part of the preparation for receiving Communion. Orthodox Copts, who insist that Communion follow Confession, expect that all family members will have the same confessor to facilitate family counseling. Other non-Catholic Easterners more commonly practice general confession, either within the liturgy or as a separate service, rather than individual confession.

- *Holy Unction:* While some Eastern Catholics have adopted, willingly or under pressure, the medieval Western practice of extreme unction in the context of "last rites," this is certainly not the traditional Eastern approach to this mystery. Byzantine and Coptic traditions, for example, call for seven priests to participate in anointing the sick, originally in the context of the Eucharist. Today, some Byzantine churches celebrate this mystery for all on Wednesday in Holy Week, when Christ's anointing by the woman at Bethany is remembered. Each Eastern Church also has other prayers and services of intercession for the sick in their ritual. In the West, this sacrament is now known as "anointing of the sick."
- *Marriage* is known among Eastern Christians as the "Mystery of Crowning"—a term taken from its principal rite, in which wreaths or crowns are placed on the heads of the couple—or, in the Assyrian and Malabar Churches, the "Blessing," as the priest's blessing is essential for the validity of this mystery in

all Eastern Churches. The mystery may not be conferred by a deacon or simply "witnessed" by a priest as in the Roman Church. The exchange of consent (written in some traditions and oral in others) and the giving of rings is actually part of the Betrothal Service, which may immediately precede the Crowning or may be held at the engagement. In the latter case jewelry and other wedding finery may be blessed, particularly in the Syriac churches. When performed on the day of the wedding, the betrothal may be held in the church narthex; then the couple enter the nave together and bring their relationship to the Lord. Many Slavic parents walk in this procession, carrying icons that will be given to the couple for their new home. Some parishes have adopted the general American practice of the father walking his daughter down the aisle to the tune of Wagner's *Bridal Chorus.*

Other wedding rites include, in Byzantine churches, a procession in which the priest leads the couple three times around the sacramental table and, in most traditions, the drinking of the "common cup" of wine. In the Assyrian and Malabar Churches, blessing with and, sometimes, conferral of the cross (in India, in place of a crown) is an important feature. Some Malabar Catholics preserve the old Assyrian practice of bathing and shaving the groom before the wedding and purifying the bridal chamber at its conclusion. In some Malankara churches, the groom covers the bride with a ritual shawl, symbolizing his promise to provide for and protect her. He may also tie around her neck—with a complicated knot—a *minnu* or amulet symbolic of the indissolubility of marriage. Middle Eastern women may conclude or even interrupt the ritual by ululating (producing a high trilling sound, thought to be connected with the word "alleluia") in response to congratulatory verses sung by a prominent family member. This may also be heard at baptisms or other occasions. People from some parts of the Middle East purposely "kidnap" the bride on the way to the church in a lighthearted attempt to tease the groom. Pastors on tight schedules are rarely amused.

- *Funeral* rites are often quite different in spirit than the general American practice. Mourning is not discouraged and traditional displays of grief are expected. All Middle Eastern women may dress in black, and men in the immediate family refrain from shaving as a sign of their loss. Wakes are often attended by representatives of every family in the community and are the site of frequent memorial services or the reading of the Psalter. The offering of incense is an important feature in the memorial services of all traditions; Maronites, for example, call this prayer the *"Incense Service."* The casket is frequently left open at the funeral service so that mourners may give the "last kiss" to the departed before the burial. In many traditions the burial is followed by the Meal of Mercy, a sometimes elaborate dinner for all attending. Traditionally this dinner, rather than the church service, was the place for eulogies by family members and friends.

  Memorial services are prescribed for certain days in the various Eastern Churches. The third, sixth, ninth, and fortieth days as well as anniversaries may be solemnized with memorial services, including the distribution of sweetened bread or a dish of boiled wheat, fruits, and nuts. Memorial services are also conducted at cemeteries on certain occasions such as the week of Easter, the various days of remembering the dead in the different traditions or, in the United States, on Memorial Day.

- *Blessings:* Eastern Christians also observe many blessings and other similar rites in connection with the birth of a child. The *churching* of a newborn on the fortieth day is one of the more popular rites and often marks the child's first journey outside the home. In Slavic churches, this service is often joined to the child's baptism. Blessings for establishing a new home, the beginning of school, or the start of a journey are frequently served. Less frequently seen but particularly moving are the rites for the adoption of a child or the establishment of a spiritual relationship in the Byzantine tradition.

The Church Year

Commentators have noted that in the United States today, church attendance is almost exclusively a Sunday affair. Some immigrants fall easily into this pattern; others cherish the feasts and fasts of the Church year and try to observe them in the face of the prevailing culture. Converts to Eastern Churches are often drawn to them because of their rich liturgical cycle.

Each tradition has its own calendar of feasts and fasting seasons that are similar to one another, but also different in many respects. We have already mentioned the discrepancy between the Julian and Gregorian calendars. Some other differences include:

- *Holy Week and Easter:* In every Eastern Church, Pascha, the Feast of the Resurrection, is the principal feast of the year, around which the calendar is organized. It is often called the "Feast of Feasts" and includes many special observances. Most Eastern Churches begin the Great and Holy Week on *Lazarus Saturday* (the day before Palm Sunday), celebrating Christ's raising of Lazarus, which precipitated his welcome on Palm Sunday. In some parts of the Middle East, children go from house to house on this day acting out the raising of Lazarus in story and song. Some parishes observe this practice, but usually on church grounds.

- *Palm Sunday* processions are especially prominent in the Middle Eastern churches, because of their proximity to the Holy Land. As in the event it commemorates, children are featured. Specially outfitted, they often carry large candles (perhaps their baptismal candles) elaborately decorated with palms, olive branches, and flowers. In northern Europe, palms were unavailable and so branches of pussy willow were blessed instead. Slavic churches in the West often use both palms and pussy willows on this day. In some Syriac churches, people throw palm branches at the "feet of Christ" when the gospel is read.

  In Maronite churches, the Holy Week begins with a rite called "Coming to the Harbor," marking the completion of the fast and the arrival at the kingdom. The first three days of the Holy Week are marked in many Byzantine churches by the *Liturgy of the Presanctified Gifts* and the celebration of the *Bridegroom Service,* actually the matins of the day, so named from a hymn sung each evening: "I see Your bridal chamber adorned, O my Savior, but I have no garment to enter therein. Brighten the robe of my soul, O Giver of light, and save me." Holy Wednesday is marked in many Byzantine parishes by the *Mystery of*

Holy Unction, called the *Service of the Lamp* in the Maronite Church.

- *On Holy Thursday,* most churches serve the Divine Liturgy commemorating the Last Supper and a matins service commemorating the arrest, trial, and death of Christ. In Byzantine churches, this story is recounted in twelve Gospel readings. In Middle Eastern churches, the priest carries a life-sized cross in procession through the darkened church, then "nails" an icon of Christ to it. The cross may be venerated through the next day. The washing of the feet is prescribed in Maronite parishes; in the Byzantine and some other Syriac churches, this rite is properly performed by the bishop.

- *Holy Friday* is observed by special services through the day. In the morning some parishes observe the "royal hours" (so called because the Byzantine emperor attended them in state) before the cross. At vespers, the body of Christ is taken from the cross and wrapped in a shroud for burial, taken in procession and placed in a tomb in the center of the church. In Byzantine churches, this holy shroud is embroidered with an icon of the dead Christ, and people may take turns keeping watch at the tomb through the night, particularly in Slavic parishes. In Middle Eastern churches, the "burial" is part of the matins service. At the end of the procession, people traditionally bend to walk under the shroud before it is placed in the tomb, then receive the flowers that bedeck the tomb. In Syriac churches, it is the cross that is sprinkled with rose water, wrapped in linen, and placed in the tomb.

- *Holy Saturday* in Byzantine churches commemorates the "harrowing of hell," Christ's descent among the dead as mentioned in 1 Peter 3:19–20. At the vesper-liturgy, before the gospel announcement of the resurrection, dark vestments and altar covers are changed for bright ones in Slavic churches, and laurel leaves are strewn about the church in Greek and Melkite churches to herald the resurrection. In the Middle East, this day is known as the "Saturday of Light," marked by baptisms in Byzantine churches and the communal reconciliation of penitents in the Maronite Church.

- *Pascha* begins with matins served at night in some parishes and at sunrise in others. In Byzantine churches, the service begins with a candlelight procession in the darkness outside the church, stopping at the church door, to recall the journey of the women at daybreak. The resurrection is announced, and people enter the brightly lit and decorated church to celebrate the new life come to the world. In Byzantine churches, the shroud is left on the altar and the doors of the icon screen are left open to suggest the empty tomb. At the Liturgy or in the evening at vespers, the gospel is read in many languages to proclaim the good news of Christ to the world. In Syriac churches, the cross, now draped festively, is carried in procession and the flowers adorning the tomb are distributed. In Byzantine churches, the *Artos*, a special loaf of bread adorned with an icon of the resurrection, is blessed after the Liturgy, as are paschal foods that people have brought to the church. In Slavic churches, these foods—the meat and dairy products from which people had abstained during the fast—are arranged in baskets with sometimes elaborately embroidered covers passed down from generation to generation. In some Romanian and Slavic parishes, members may meet during the fast to prepare the intricately decorated eggs called *pysanky,* which are treasured items in many homes. Among Middle Eastern Christians, the eggs are colored red in honor of the blood of Christ. People crack the eggs against one another, recalling Christ's emergence from the tomb, as they exchange the greeting ("Christ is risen—Indeed He is risen"). Many parishes have festive gatherings either on Pascha itself or on the following Sunday.

Other Feast Days

The important events in the mystery of the incarnation are celebrated in many Eastern Churches as the "Twelve Great Feasts." There are some similarities with Western holy days but many differences as well, as there are among the different Eastern Churches. These twelve holy days include:

1. *Palm Sunday*
2. September 8: *Nativity of the Mother of God*
3. September 13/14: *Exaltation of the Holy Cross* (On this day special processions with a decorated cross are held and the four directions of the compass blessed. Flowers or, in some Middle Eastern Churches, branches of sweet basil are distributed.)
4. November 21: *Entrance of the Mother of God into the Temple*
5. December 25: *Nativity of Christ* (In Slavic parishes, the eves of Christmas and the Theophany may be marked with a "Holy Supper" consisting of twelve meatless courses, followed by the celebration of great compline.)
6. January 6: *Holy Theophany* (Recalls the manifestation of the Trinity on the occasion of Christ's

baptism in the Jordan River. On this day water is blessed in the church and distributed. In Slav Byzantine churches, a triple candle, representing the Trinity, is plunged into the water. Maronites purify the water by immersing in it a burning coal from the censer. Homes are blessed with this water, and the priest may go from house to house for this blessing on the occasion of this feast. If there is a river or stream nearby, another blessing is held there. In the cold of northern Europe, with rivers frozen on this date, a custom arose of blessing crosses made of ice.)

7. February 2: *The Encounter* (Recalls Christ's meeting with his people in the persons of Simeon and Anna as recorded in Luke 2:22-38. In some churches, candles are blessed and distributed on this day in honor of "the Light enlightening the Gentiles," as Simeon called him.)

8. March 25: *The Annunciation*

9. *Ascension Thursday*

10. *Pentecost* (Once called the *rosalia* or feast of flowers, this feast celebrates the life of the Spirit in the Church. Slavs adorn their churches and often their homes with greenery on this day in celebration of this new life. In Byzantine and Syriac churches, the "Prayers of Kneeling" are observed during vespers or at the Liturgy to mark the end of Paschaltide and the resumption of kneeling for prayer. In the Syriac churches, water is also blessed on this day and the people are sprinkled with it to recall how the Living Water of the Spirit was first poured out upon the faithful.)

11. August 6: *The Transfiguration of Christ* (On this day grapes and, in Slavic churches, other fruit are

blessed and distributed. Grapes, which can be transformed into wine and then into the Blood of Christ in the Eucharist, have come to be associated with Christ, the Source of our transformation. This feast is observed in the Armenian tradition on the Fourteenth Sunday after Easter.)

12. August 15: *The Dormition (Repose) of the Mother of God* (In some Byzantine churches a Burial Service for the Holy Virgin, patterned on that of Good Friday, may be held. In Slavic churches flowers are blessed on this day.)

- *Lesser feasts of Christ* include the *Circumcision* (January 1 in Byzantine and Syriac churches) and the *Mandylion,* or Icon of Christ Made without Hands, the veil imprinted with the image of Christ and brought to the city of Edessa early in the Christian era (August 16). On the Third Sunday of the Great Fast, Byzantine churches keep a special commemoration of the cross to encourage perseverance in the efforts of the season. Similarly, Syriac churches remember the temptation of Christ on the middle Wednesday of the fast.
- *Other Marian feasts* include a remembrance of her maternity on the day (or Friday) after Christmas and, in Byzantine churches, the *Protection of the Mother of God* (October 1). Syriac churches invoke Mary as patroness of the Sowing or Seeds on May 15. In the Eastern Churches, the conception of the Mother of God is actually kept as a feast of Saint Ann (December 9), just as the conception of Christ is a feast of his mother. Most Eastern Catholics took up the Western focus of this feast in the nineteenth century.

• Besides the Feast of the Holy Cross, there are a number of commemorations in the Eastern Churches connected to the *life and history of the Church.* Syriac churches begin the liturgical year eight weeks before Christmas with one or two "Sundays of the Church." Altar appointments are removed, the church blessed with holy water and incense, and new appointments set out to mark the new year. Byzantine churches commemorate the seven ecumenical councils of the first millennium on Sundays in July and October as well as the Sunday before Pentecost. The restoration of icons at the end of the iconoclast controversy is celebrated with a special procession and veneration of icons on the First Sunday of the Great Fast, the Sunday of Orthodoxy.

The Fasts

Many Eastern Christians retain the custom of fasting during each week for much of the year on Fridays and for most, on Wednesdays as well, as outlined in the first-century *Didache.* Traditionally, fasting means not eating or drinking for a prescribed time (until noon in the Middle East), then, when one does eat, avoiding meat, fish, and dairy. In this way people show their desire to return to communion with God by eating the "food of Paradise" (the produce of the Earth), as noted in Genesis. The degree of fasting, prescribed for monastics, is held up as a goal for all believers without the sense of obligation long common in the West. Many Eastern Catholics, however, have absorbed the Western attitudes and methods of fasting. There are also at least four fasting seasons through the year in the tradition of the East. Eastern Church fasts include:

- *The Great Fast:* Comparable to Lent in the West, although the forty days are computed differently. The Great Fast begins two days before Ash Wednesday and ends exactly forty days later, the day before Lazarus Saturday. In addition to fasting itself, the season is marked by special services including, in Byzantine churches, the Vespers of Forgiveness, the Liturgy of the Presanctified Gifts, and great compline. Some churches include in their lenten schedules the singing of *akathists* (lengthy liturgical poems with popular refrains) to the Mother of God or to the Divine Passion. At the Vespers of Forgiveness, which begins the season, everyone asks pardon of everyone else for any offense they may have committed so that the season can begin in purity. In some churches, this day is called "Clean Monday." The Liturgy of the Presanctified Gifts is a combination of vespers and a Communion service held on the evening of fast days. In Byzantine churches, the joy of the Divine Liturgy is considered inappropriate to fast days, and the reserved Eucharist, sanctified on the previous Sunday, is given at this service.

  In Maronite churches, vespers *(ramsho)* on Fridays includes the veneration of the holy cross. Syriac parishes have a Presanctified Liturgy on Fridays called the "Signing of the Chalice." Maronites observe this only on Good Friday. The season is divided into three cycles: a three-week penitential cycle, two "Weeks of Miracles," and a "Week of Palms" preceding Palm Sunday. In many parishes, lenten suppers consisting of vegetarian foods are held, often as fundraisers for charitable projects.

- *The Nativity Fast:* Varies in length in different traditions. In Byzantine churches, it is marked by the celebration of several days in honor of the Old Testament prophets and ancestors of Christ. In Syriac churches, the season is built around New Testament events preceding Christ's birth, such as the Annunciation, and the conception and birth of John the Baptist. Maronites observe the nine days preceding Christmas with a special service in memory of the nine months Christ spent in his mother's womb. The Armenians observe three weeks of fasting (the first, third, and last weeks of their fifty-day pre-Christmas season).

- *The Fast of Nineveh:* Observed in some Syriac churches, a three-day fast between the Theophany and the Great Fast, followed by a day of thanksgiving.
- *The Fast of Peter and Paul:* Following Pentecost, but of varying length in different traditions.
- *The Fast of the Mother of God:* The first fourteen days of August, preceding the Feast of the Dormition. In some Byzantine churches, the Paraclisis Service, a devotion to the Holy Virgin, is served frequently during this season.

The Saints

Every Eastern Church has its own saints whom it remembers with special devotion. They may be remembered more on local calendars or in churches dedicated to their memory than universally. Each tradition has a Feast of All Saints, but on different dates. In Byzantine churches, this feast is held on the Sunday after Pentecost. Some Eastern Catholics have incorporated into their calendars the feasts of some saints popular in the West.

The Dead

Universal commemorations of the departed are found in every tradition. Byzantine churches observe two or more

"Saturdays of the Dead" during the pre-lenten, lenten, and paschal seasons. In some Syriac churches, the last three Sundays after the Theophany are "Sundays of the Departed," remembering priests, righteous (the saints), and all believers successively. Assyrians observe this memorial on the last Friday before the Great Fast.

Scripture Readings

Each Church has its own lectionary, or cycle of Scripture readings appointed through the year. Byzantine churches have a cycle of continuous readings for Sundays, Saturdays, and weekdays of the year punctuated by special readings on feast days. In Syriac churches, there are as many as five readings from the Old and New Testaments at the Divine Liturgy. In Byzantine churches, the Old Testament readings are found in vespers during the Great Fast and on certain feasts.

What's Missing?

The circumstances of daily life for Eastern Christians in America are very different from their countries of origin. In some matters, their lives are much easier in the West than elsewhere. Christians who lived with a daily fear of arrest under the Soviets, of discrimination in Israel, or of mob oppression in some Islamic countries welcome the freedom they find in the West. Other aspects of Christian life, even when lived under difficult circumstances, are missed by Christians, whether they can articulate them or not. Some of these elements not found in this country include:

- *Large-scale gatherings of Christians:* Particularly in countries where Christians are a minority, demonstrations, particularly on the Great Feasts of Pascha and the Theophany, are important in the life of the

Church. They are statements of the continued existence of Christianity and vigor under Islam or Hinduism. Thousands gather for the public announcement of the resurrection or the blessing of water. Fireworks and volleys of gunshots echo through towns and villages. There is no doubt that the Christians are celebrating the presence of Christ in the world.

In contrast, American Christians keep their celebrations within the four walls of their churches. Even on the greatest feasts, there are few attempts to mark the importance of the day for Christian life with any kind of public celebration. More often than not, American church exteriors are not adorned in any way on Easter. While some Protestants may plan common sunrise services, Western Catholics rarely vary their ordinary Sunday schedules.

- *Notable shrines:* Most Eastern Christians come from countries with a 1,000- or 2,000-year Christian history. While many churches have been destroyed over the centuries, people are never far from places sanctified by centuries of prayer. Often these holy places shelter the tombs of saints or miraculous icons where healings and other miracles have been recorded. People visit them regularly and often go to them for baptisms and other rites. Feasts of these saints are likely observed in their shrines as regional feasts to which people come from miles around. In America there are few such holy places; what shrines do exist have little interest for Eastern Christians; they certainly do not bear witness to the faith of the immigrants' ancestors who prayed at them for generation after generation.

The average believer needs, from time to time, an experience of the wider Church. Diocesan or inter-parish gatherings reinforce the ordinary Christian's sense of belonging to a widespread community of faith. While most Eastern Christians hold diocese-wide conventions or pilgrimages, the great geographical distance covered by each diocese limits the number of participants in such gatherings. The Orthodox Churches attempt to hold such gatherings on a regional, interdiocesan basis, particularly on the Sunday of Orthodoxy. For the most part, Eastern Catholics have yet to adopt a similar policy.

- *Daily access to the church:* Most Eastern Catholics came from areas in which the people lived quite close to their churches. People walking around town would stop into a church for a moment of prayer or to light a candle. The church was accessible to them even when no gathering was scheduled. In contrast, there are few places in the United States where people walk anywhere! Should someone pull into the church parking lot, they would like as not find the church locked for insurance purposes, except for those churches that promote Eucharistic adoration. Since Eastern Christians may live an hour away from their own churches, they are even less likely to seek out a moment of prayer in their church.

- *Monasteries and spiritual guides:* Every Eastern Christian Church abroad has its monastic centers where people come to request prayers or to seek spiritual guidance from elders with recognized spiritual authority. As Pope John Paul II noted in his encyclical, *Orientale Lumen,* all Eastern Churches have seen the ascetic life of monastics as the deepest experience of the Christian life and look to monastics to provide the spiritual and also the hierarchical leadership of the Church. Monastics in these Churches follow centuries-old spiritual traditions, often in the same places where renowned ascetics lived before them.

Several Orthodox Churches in America, notably the Copts and the Greeks, have imported monastics from Mount Athos or the Egyptian desert to make a beginning for monastic life in this country. Eastern Catholics, on the other hand, have few true monasteries, having preferred the para-monastic life of Western-inspired congregations. The leadership of the Eastern Catholic Churches needs to develop strategies for encouraging monastic life in several areas of the country so that their members can cultivate an awareness of and desire for a deeper spiritual life. Besides the ordinary liturgical assembly and the large-group experiences of pilgrimages and conventions, believers need more intimate experiences of the Church, exemplified by contact with monastics and the privacy of quiet moments in a neighborhood church. The development of small groups for study and prayer in the tradition may be a contemporary approach to meet this need.

The Church down the Block

It is the rare Eastern Catholic who does not drive past two or three Roman Catholic parish complexes before arriving at his or her own parish church. Often Eastern Catholics simply attend the church closest to their home, out of convenience, or because the Eastern Catholic's spouse comes from a Western background and is more comfortable in a Western church. Being in communion means that Eastern and Western Catholics can freely and fully worship in one another's churches. Occasionally, however, some Eastern

Catholics simply feel that the Roman Church is the "American" Church and that one aspect of becoming American is to worship in such a church. Some Greek Catholics from the Middle East, where they are called *Room Catholeek* (Roman Catholics—referring to Constantinople, the "New Rome"), occasionally think that the Roman Church is their Church in the West, particularly since, in the Middle East, Western Catholics are not called "Roman" or even "Catholic," but *Lateen* (Latins).

The canon law of both Eastern and Western Churches directs that, wherever an Eastern Catholic eparchy or parish is established, Eastern Catholics come under its jurisdiction, and children baptized in any Catholic tradition would be considered members of the father's historic Church. The marriage involving an Eastern Catholic and a non–Roman Catholic blessed in a Roman Catholic Church would be canonically invalid if a parish of the Eastern Catholic's own tradition was accessible. While Eastern Catholics should be actively seeking out their own people, Roman Catholic clergy and parish workers should also be sensitive to these issues as well. Persons with Indian, Slavic, or Middle Eastern names should be asked about any possible Eastern background and referred to any nearby Eastern Catholic parish. This may avoid canonical problems in certain cases, but in every instance it would strengthen the witness of Eastern parishes to the universality of the Catholic communion of Churches.

Another discrepancy between Eastern and Western Catholic canons concerns transferring to another Catholic Church on the occasion of a marriage. According to Western canon law,[2] a spouse, on entering marriage or at any time during its course, may simply declare that he or she is transferring to the autonomous Church of the other spouse. This means that a Roman Catholic man may transfer to the Church of his Eastern Catholic wife by simply making his wishes known to his pastor. According to the Eastern canons,[3] however, it is only a wife who may effect such a transfer. The culture and civil laws of many Eastern countries dictate that in law a wife follow her husband.

The Problem of Catholic Schools

A frequently cited reason why Eastern Catholics may join a Roman Catholic parish despite accessibility to their own church is their desire to send their children to a Catholic school. Eastern Catholics have long been accustomed to attending Catholic schools, particularly in areas where Christians are a minority. They value the Catholic school's ability to support their Christian identity in a sea of Hindus or Muslims. Some Eastern Catholic schools were established in the United States but became less and less viable as people moved farther from the "old neighborhood." Few people would drive their children to a school across town when another was close by.

Most Catholic schools in the United States are a ministry of specific Roman Catholic parishes. This is not the case in some other countries, where schools may be attached to monasteries or religious communities rather than parishes. School and parish functions would be clearly separate, especially where Catholic schools also educate members of various Orthodox Churches. Often in the United States, Eastern Catholic parents are or, at least, feel pressured to join a Roman Catholic parish to obtain a place in the parish school for their child. Still other parents feel that joining the parish would be good economics because parishioners receive an automatic discount on tuition. Still others have been accustomed in their homelands to feel obligated to join whatever church provides them with any kind of social service.

Once in the parish school, other issues develop. Without specific direction to the contrary, teachers and principals naturally try to incorporate all Catholic children into the parish sacramental programs. Educators may expect Eastern Catholics—knowingly or inadvertently—to repeat certain sacraments of initiation (confirmation or First Communion). Some parents may encourage their participation as a social milestone or so that their children will not feel left out; others may simply not realize that these sacraments should not be repeated. School authorities and parish clergy need to know the sacramental status of Eastern Catholic students in their schools and to see that these sacraments are not repeated. The American Catholic bishops have directed that Eastern Catholic students who have not received these sacraments should receive them in their own proper Church:

> If, at the time of confirmation for the class or group of children in the sacramental program, it is found that a child belonging to an Eastern Church has not yet received the holy mystery of Chrismation, the child must then be chrismated in his or her proper autonomous ritual Church.... Children of Eastern Catholic Churches who have not received the Eucharist at the time of their Christian initiation, should receive their first Holy Communion in their own autonomous Church.[4]

Sensitive Roman Catholic clergy and educators also need to learn the sacramental discipline of Eastern Catholics in their midst and respect it. Some churches chrismate children at baptism but do not give them the Eucharist. Others admit all the baptized of whatever age to Eucharistic communion. Parents from the latter traditions often report that

Roman Catholic clergy refuse to communicate their younger children even though they have already been initiated into this mystery in their own Church.

In 1999, the Oriental Orthodox-Roman Catholic Theological Consultation in the United States developed *Guidelines Concerning the Pastoral Care of Oriental Orthodox Students in Catholic Schools.* It suggested some resources for acquiring knowledge of these Churches and their traditions. The Guidelines addressed two of the issues described earlier:

> As a matter of principle, the Catholic Church does not seek converts among the faithful of the Oriental Orthodox Churches. Thus every effort should be made to respect and even promote the participation of Oriental Orthodox students in the life of their own churches, and to avoid practices that could appear to constitute an invitation for an Oriental Orthodox student to join the Catholic Church. In particular, it is inappropriate for Oriental Orthodox students to be included in preparation programs for Confirmation or First Communion, especially since they will have received these sacraments at the time of their baptism.[5]

The Oriental Orthodox-Catholic Guidelines also addressed the issue of the financial incentive in joining the Roman Catholic parish that maintains a parochial school:

> Another practice that can give the impression of seeking converts is the requirement in some places of membership in—and financial contributions to—the Catholic parish where a school is located in order to pay a lower tuition fee. This can appear to be a financial incentive for an Oriental

Orthodox family to join the Catholic parish. While the tuition policy of Catholic schools is a complex question and we cannot offer a solution to this problem that would be applicable in all cases, we strongly encourage Catholic pastors to find a way to allow Oriental Orthodox to participate in their schools without appearing to encourage transfer of membership to the sponsoring Catholic parish.[6]

This course of action, as we have shown, is even more desirable in the case of Eastern Catholics, the maintenance of whose heritage has been so strongly urged in papal and conciliar documents. Pastors and parish leaders who attempt to put this guideline in practice are surely the particular friends of Christian unity.

Notes

1. This material has appeared in several variations in a number of different publications such as Frederica Mathewes-Green, *At the Corner of East and Now* (New York: Jeremy P. Tarcher/Putnam, 1999), pp. 269–275.

2. *Code of Canon Law* [of the Western Church] (Washington, DC: CLSA Publications, 1983), can. 112, §2.

3. *Code of Canons of the Eastern Churches* (Washington, DC: CLSA Publications, 1992), can. 32.

4. Committee on the Relationship between Eastern and Latin Catholic Churches, *Eastern Catholics in the United States of America* (Washington, DC: United States Catholic Conference, 1999), 28–29.

5. Oriental Orthodox-Roman Catholic Theological Consultation in the United States, *Guidelines Concerning the Pastoral Care of Oriental Orthodox Students in Catholic Schools* (Washington DC: United States Catholic Conference, 1999), ¶4.

6. Ibid., 5.

Chapter 5

CONTEMPORARY CHALLENGES

ISSUES CONFRONTING EASTERN CATHOLICS IN AMERICAN SOCIETY

In 1964, the late Father Alexander Schmemann, inspirer of pastoral liturgy in Eastern Orthodox and Byzantine Catholic Churches throughout the world, wrote a series of articles for *St. Vladimir's Seminary Quarterly* on "Problems of Orthodoxy in America." In them he evaluated the canonical, liturgical, and spiritual situation of the Churches of his day. He described as the canonical problem the multiplicity of Orthodox jurisdictions in the United States, largely based on allegiance to various mother Churches abroad. This he contrasted to the historic principle of Church unity—"one city, one bishop"—noting that, prior to 1917, the vast majority of Orthodox in America had been part of a single jurisdiction. These divisions, he reasoned, must adversely affect any attempts to evangelize America.

Reflecting on the liturgical problems of his day, Father Schmemann pinpointed the question of effective liturgical formation, rather than issues of language, translations, or rubrics, as the principal challenge facing the Church. People who are not motivated to live the liturgy will ignore it in whatever language or in whatever style it may be practiced.

He saw a pressing spiritual problem for the Orthodox to be the parochialization of Christian life: the Church was reduced to "my parish" and living the life in Christ to being a "parishioner in good standing." These same problems, in one form or another, affected Eastern Catholics as well as Orthodox and still challenge their Churches today.

Canonical Issues

At the time Father Schmemann wrote his articles, the Eastern Catholic canonical problem was not a multiplicity of jurisdictions but a lack of them. There were only two Eastern Catholic jurisdictions in the United States: the Ukrainian Greek Catholic archdiocese of Philadelphia with one suffragan eparchy, and two Ruthenian eparchies directly dependent on Rome. Armenian, Maronite, Melkite, Romanian, and Russian parishes, established at roughly the same time as the first Slavic communities, were subject to the Roman Catholic bishops in whose dioceses they were situated. Circumstances in their homelands had yet to prompt any sizeable immigration of other Eastern Catholics at that time.

Since then the four Ruthenian and Ukrainian eparchies have been divided into eight, and the Ruthenian eparchies have been united in an archdiocese, which is now considered an autonomous *(sui juris)* metropolitan Church. Eparchies have been created for most of the other Eastern Catholic communities, facilitating the establishment of parishes for their members across the country. These communities were no longer dependent on the goodwill (or lack thereof) of bishops who knew little of their tradition. They were, for example, no longer obliged to conform to standards of parish size that made sense in the Roman Catholic community but that kept many smaller Eastern Catholic communities from being established. This contrasted with the practice of the

Orthodox Churches, which regularly organized communities of thirty or forty families and helped build churches for them.

The establishment of Eastern Catholic eparchies in America also gave these communities a canonical status they did not have before. All, however, are dependent on Rome in much the same way as Roman Catholic dioceses, including those that have ties to a mother Church. Thus, the Chaldean and Maronite eparchies for the eastern and western United States have no connection among themselves; their bishops are part of synods in the mother Churches abroad, which rarely address issues affecting their eparchies around the world.

Connection to a Church abroad has the value of maintaining unity with the historic centers of Eastern Christianity. The kind of ethnic identification that it fosters retards the spread and growth of these eparchies. It inhibits existing communities from reaching out to parishes of different ethnic backgrounds that share the same spiritual tradition. Thus the ten Greek Catholic eparchies, which preserve the usages of four mother Churches in the Middle East and Eastern Europe, often strain personnel and material resources to maintain parishes in the same neighborhood. Sometimes there are two or more of these churches on the same street when one church served by a priest conversant with each usage would suffice. There has been no organized attempt at addressing any of these issues in any kind of shared way among Eastern Catholics, although it is one of the more easily remedied structural challenges faced by Eastern Catholics of similar liturgical traditions.

Bishops of all the Eastern Catholic Churches in the United States have established an organization for sharing and common action called the Eastern Catholic Associates. Although without any canonical status, it has provided a vehicle for some common action, particularly in the area of religious education. It sponsors an organization, the Eastern

Catholic Diocesan Directors of Religious Education (ECDD), and a catechetical publishing arm, God With Us Publications, that issues religious education material for Eastern Catholics in America, such as the three-volume series, *Light for Life,* the adult catechism of the Greek Catholic eparchies in America.

A similar attempt at sharing has been the regional "Fraternal Encounters" of Eastern Catholic bishops and other leadership initiated by the Vatican Congregation for the Eastern Catholic Churches. The first of these brought together hierarchs from the Western Hemisphere and Oceania in 1999 to discuss common problems. A second encounter, for bishops in English-speaking countries, was held in 2006.

Eastern Catholics in different parts of the United States have taken the opportunity for regional gatherings and associations of various kinds. An important example is the Eastern Catholic Pastoral Association of Southern California, which brings together clergy and religious from the Armenian, Assyrian-Chaldean, Ruthenian, Coptic, Maronite, Melkite, Romanian, Russian, Syriac, and Ukrainian Catholic Churches. The association provides a forum of fellowship and discussion among members, addresses issues of common concern touching on the local Eastern Churches and on ecumenical affairs, and makes available information about the Eastern Catholic Churches.

Liturgical and Spiritual Issues

Since the 1960s there has been a considerable interest among Eastern Catholics in appropriating more of their liturgical heritage. Liturgical texts—formerly available only in Greek, Slavonic, or Syriac—have been translated into English and provided with musical settings. Services that had fallen into disuse in periods of latinization—such as vespers and matins *(orthros)* or the Liturgy of the Presanctified Gifts in the Byzantine eparchies and *ramsho* and *sapro* (morning and evening prayer) in the Syriac churches—have been restored to use in many parishes.

At the same time, however, the most pressing liturgical problem identified by Father Schmemann remains and, if anything, has become more widespread. In too many places and for too great a percentage of parishioners, the liturgical life has been replaced in parishes, he noted, by activities, meetings, trips, and organizations.[1] The power of the liturgy to influence lives, he asserted, "has all but vanished." In many instances, liturgy and spirituality had become irrelevant to parish life, which focused on dinner dances, fundraisers, and other "club" activities rather than on the possibility of communion with God.

Even among more recent immigrants, many of whom continue to pray, fast, and read the Bible privately, communal worship features less and less in their religious life. For many of them, coming to church was chiefly an opportunity to identify with other believers in the only setting that was exclusively theirs, in contrast to the Islamic, Jewish, or Hindu society surrounding them. Their church attendance may have been more a result of its place as the focus of the Christian community than of their commitment to a liturgical way of life. Unfortunately, few pastors are able to see that without a solid spiritual formation, people will simply not continue attending church because it is something they've always done. Alas, ongoing formation is still not the norm in too many Eastern Catholic Churches.

Secularism versus the Church as Way of Life

The root cause underlying all these symptoms, Father Schmemann indicated, is the secularism inherent in the

American way of life. "The basic aspects of human existence," he wrote, "such as family, education, science, profession, art, etc. are not only not rooted in or related to religious faith, but the very necessity or possibility of such correlation is denied."[2] He quoted Will Herberg's observation that "America seems to be at once the most religious and the most secular of nations," observing certain isolated religious practices but absorbing values that are not informed by religious principles.

Father Schmemann noted that it is often the most active parishioners who are the first to claim that it is impossible to live an Orthodox lifestyle here. By this they may mean that it is "impossible" to observe the cycle of feasts and fasts of their Church. But they may equally mean that is "impossible" to follow the precepts of the gospel, that these teachings were fine for "back then" but are impractical now and, therefore, do not apply.

Thus, many have simply fallen into a secular way of life while maintaining a minimum of religious practice. They may attend church from time to time but the "gospel" they follow is written and produced by the media, their "pilgrimages" are to Las Vegas or Atlantic City, and their "spiritual guides" are the pundits of late-night television. They have appropriated the values of our secular society—success, security, affluence, competition, status, profit, prestige, ambition—and fail to recognize that they are the values of "this age."[3]

Others lament this situation and feel they have not realized their aspirations in America. As one Eastern Catholic, an immigrant from a dominantly Islamic society, told me, "I thought we were coming to a Christian country, but the religion of this country is business." They find it difficult to realize that Christian commitment here is more a matter of individual choice than of societal convention. It is difficult for people from many Eastern societies to realize that religious observance in the West must be more a matter of personal conviction than communal practice.

In contrast, the realization that the mores of society made it difficult to observe the Christian life historically prompted the creation of "alternative societies": monastic communities or lay brotherhoods. While some Orthodox Churches have made deliberate attempts to organize monastic life of the traditional models, their Eastern Catholic counterparts have been less committed to the need for the monastic witness in their Churches. In his 1995 Apostolic Letter on the Eastern Churches, *Orientale Lumen,* Pope John Paul II described Eastern monasticism as "the very soul of the Eastern Churches," "a reference point for all the baptized," and a "prophetic place where creation becomes praise of God and the precept of concretely lived charity becomes the ideal of human coexistence."[4] The Eastern Catholic Churches in America have yet to make their own these inspiring words of the pope.

Religion as a Community Expression

Eastern Catholics, particularly those from Asian or Middle Eastern societies, have more of a difficulty than, say, Western European immigrants in expressing their faith in a secular society. They come from traditions in which public religious practice is often more a communal than an individual requirement. It is the community, more than the individual, that is obliged to celebrate the Liturgy and offices of the Lord's Day. The Liturgy is primarily the public witness of the royal priesthood to God's saving plan rather than a private "obligation." In these communities an individual might regret missing Sunday Mass on occasion but not consider it a "mortal sin," as the Liturgy is still being served by the community. The Church recognizes this and prays for "those who are absent for reasonable causes."[5] But if the "community," that is, the greater society, observes no religion and honors no holy day, Easterners may be more likely to follow along. After all, this is the "American way."

Even in those countries where Christians are a minority, compared to Hindus, Jews, or Muslims, each community publicly observes its own feasts and fasts. The state and other religious groups respect and publicly acknowledge one another's practices. Thus, Muslim civil officials, including heads of state, regularly attend Christian Christmas and Easter services out of regard for the Christian communities in their nations. Each community may have its own beliefs and traditions, but the state recognizes the fact that the entire life of all its people is based around their respective faith expressions. This may explain why recent Muslim immigrants in New York have consciously chosen to live among Orthodox Jews, because they see both communities expressing religious values in the midst of a society they each perceive as godless. In contrast, Westerners say that religion is each person's private business and does not really belong in the public arena, reflecting the American "ideal" of the separation of church and state. This is incomprehensible from an Eastern perspective.

This contrast is further complicated for those coming from Islamic countries by the institution known as "Personal Statutes." In these countries, all legal matters concerning birth, death, marriage, and inheritance are handled by Church courts. Since the state follows Islamic law, Christians would approach their own diocesan authorities for these matters, according to the laws of their respective communities. It is not obvious to many people coming from Islamic countries that in our secular society all these questions are handled by the state for all citizens. People cannot understand, for example, why they need to get a marriage license from the state since they have already filled out forms with their priest. Not a few couples have been turned away from the altar on their wedding day because they had never applied for a civil marriage license!

This understanding of religious practice as a communal expression is tied to the relational nature of traditional societies. In most cultures other than modern Western societies, people's identities are derived from their relationships within the communities, however small, to which they belong: family, clan, tribe, Church. People take their names from their relationships: Slavs are identified by relationship to their fathers and are traditionally addressed by patronymics. Even Vladimir Lenin (1870–1924) was known as Vladimir Ilyich (son of Ilya). This was once true throughout Western Europe as well, as with the Anglo-Saxon John-sons or Fitz-Williams and their Scandinavian counterparts. In the Middle East, people are known by their parents' names (*Ibn-so-and-so:* Son of so-and-so) or by their children's names: *Abu-so-and-so* or *Um-so-and-so* (so-and-so's Father or Mother). This applies to kings and presidents as well as farmers and laborers. Thus, longtime Syrian President Hafez al-Assad was regularly addressed as *Abu-Basil* (Basil's Father). One cannot imagine an American president being addressed in this way.

We live in a society in which people find their identity in what they do for a living, a practice that even some Western Europeans find offensive. The sacraments, however, and what they express are derived from a society in which relationships were paramount. In baptism, we become adopted children of the Father, a concept with less meaning in our society than in one where relationships are more highly valued. Biblical images such as the vine and the branches, the body of Christ, and the communion in the Holy Spirit have lost much of their power in Western societies that stress individuality over communal ties. The sacraments came to be seen as channels of grace between God and me rather than as corporate actions. The difficulty in restoring a communal understanding of the sacraments in a society in which religion is a private affair is known in all sacramental Churches.

The great challenge for Eastern Christian Churches, then, is to help their people see that secularism is really a religion of its own and that the burden of maintaining their faith and their church structures in this secular society falls on *them*. These Churches must also accept the challenge of making their faith expressions public in a society that too often knows them simply for their food festivals.

Consumerism versus Hospitality

Recent immigrants from all over the world to the industrial countries regularly support their families at home, often for many years. They may send a good percentage of their income abroad to raise the standard of living and provide for the future of their younger relatives. At the same time, however, there are many who quickly succumb to the lure of consumerism and dedicate themselves to owning what everyone around them does. It is not unusual for relatively new immigrants to hoard groceries and other items that they will never use. The woman who, a few years ago, bought ten identical blouses for her daughter, only to give them to our parish clothing drive unopened when the style did not please the girl, is not atypical.

Much has been written about the clash between Christian values and the consumerism rampant in much of American society. Church leaders of both East and West have challenged their members to reflect on this problem of the modern world. In a 2002 joint statement entitled "God Has Not Abandoned the World," Pope John Paul II and the Ecumenical Patriarch Bartholomew I emphasized that in succumbing to consumerism we "are betraying the mandate God has given us: to be stewards, called to collaborate with God in watching over creation in holiness and wisdom." They called for an inner change of heart "which can lead to a change in lifestyle and in unsustainable patterns of consumption and production."

It is particularly jarring to see this conspicuous consumption unquestioned in Eastern Christian communities, given the importance of hospitality in the tradition of these Churches. The revered founder of Canada's Madonna House apostolate, Catherine Doherty, witnessed to the significance of Christian hospitality among Eastern Christians in a memorable way. Describing her upbringing as the daughter of a prerevolutionary Russian nobleman in the tsar's diplomatic corps, Catherine wrote:

> Early in my childhood, the truth that Christ is in my neighbor was shown to me by my parents' example and words. No one was ever turned from our door, bum or beggar, woman of the streets or thief. The men were welcomed by my father. He gave them a bath, himself, or Mother would do it for the women; then they would be given clothing if they needed it. They would be served by Mother and Father and by us children—*if we had been good through the week,* and thus worthy of serving Christ in the poor—on our best linen and from our best china in the main dining room.[6]

The principle guiding hospitality in an Eastern Christian home is based on Saint Paul's teaching in 2 Corinthians 9:8: "And God is able to provide you with every blessing in abundance, so that by always having enough of everything, you may share abundantly in every good work." Paul distinguishes between what believers need for their sustenance and the "abundance"—the surplus not required to provide for their needs—that is meant to be shared. The Byzantine Churches pray for this kind of prosperity in the Mystery of Crowning (marriage). In the rite's first prayer the priest asks, "Fill their storehouses with wheat, wine and oil and with every good thing, that they may in turn bestow them on the needy." In the second prayer he continues, "That, having a sufficiency of everything, they may abound in every good work that is acceptable to You." From the first day of their marriage, then, the Eastern Christian couple is called to devote their resources to hospitality. The Churches' challenge in this regard is to see that families grapple with the contrast between its vision and that of our commercially motivated society.

The Challenge to Mission

The gospel records that, before his ascension, Christ sent forth his disciples to evangelize: "Go therefore and make disciples of all nations, baptizing them in the name of the Father and of the Son and of the Holy Spirit, and teaching them to obey everything that I have commanded you. And remember, I am with you always, to the end of the age" (Matt 28:19–20). Over the next few years the apostles struggled with the implication of this mission to "all nations." Under the guidance of the Holy Spirit they concluded that the Church was meant to include more than just their own fellow Jews.

For much of the second millennium, evangelism among Eastern Christians was forbidden under Islamic rule. Perhaps the sole Eastern Christian missionary Church in that era was the Russian Orthodox Church, which brought Christianity through northern Asia as far as Alaska. In addition, Eastern Catholics were long discouraged and even forbidden by Roman Catholic authorities from carrying out this mandate. Catholic evangelization was the business of the Latin Church and, oddly, many Eastern Catholics accepted this anomaly unquestioningly.

Others have embraced a more open approach to those around them. In his first pastoral letter to the Melkite Greek Catholic Eparchy of Newton in 1971, Archbishop Joseph Tawil advised:

> One day all of our ethnic traits—language, folklore, customs—will have disappeared. Time itself is seeing to this. And so we cannot think of our communities as ethnic parishes, primarily for the service of the immigrant or ethnically oriented, unless we wish to assure the death of our community. Our Churches are not only for our own people but are also for any of our fellow Americans who are attracted to our traditions which show forth the beauty of the universal Church and the variety of its riches.[7]

In America, many Eastern Catholic communities have welcomed people drawn to their parishes, whether by marriage to parishioners or by the witness of their liturgical life. As a result, these parishes number among their members people of every race and ethnic background. They are, as much as any other church community, miniatures of the wider American population.

Unfortunately, in other places inquirers have been met with suspicion: "Why are you here—you are not one of us?" Immigrants of any background who see their churches as their enclave in an otherwise foreign world may fear the loss of this refuge when others "dilute" their community. They see their role as keeping the immigrant community together, although changing property values, work patterns, and personal inclinations invariably render that goal a futile one. All churches need *open* doors to attract potential members, not *closed* doors to keep current members in. For that to happen, parishes need to gradually minimize the identification of their parishes with any one ethnic group or culture. One of the challenges that Church leaders face is devising ways to help their parishes become welcoming communities to any who might wish to share their life.

Not infrequently these same Church leaders, who do receive others who come to them, are reluctant to establish missions without a base community from their own ethnic background. When approached, they want to know how many of "our people" are involved in the move to establish a mission. They may even be reluctant to sponsor a community of Eastern Catholics of different backgrounds lest someone question their right to do so. Certainly Eastern Catholics, clergy and laity alike, have not been formed with a sense of mission to the world at large. The challenge for leaders here is to embrace Christ's commission and to find ways of giving their members the desire for mission and the tools needed to render it effective.

Affirming Diversity in a Shrinking World

Eastern Catholics in America might seem particularly suited to meet one decidedly twenty-first-century challenge facing all Christians: the rapid expansion of technology, particularly the almost instant expansion of communications throughout the world, resulting in a phenomenon termed "globalization" by world leaders. Most people welcome the access to information this technological revolution has produced. The worldwide broadcast of popular dissent at the 2004 Ukrainian presidential election influenced the turnout of national elections in Iraq and the change of government in Lebanon a few months later—events unthinkable just a few years earlier.

At the same time, Christian leaders have been warning against the dangers of globalization for the past forty years. Large financial conglomerates now operate worldwide, bringing large profits to a few in the industrial world while lowering the standards of living for the working class. Others seek to use worldwide communications and commerce to make humanity one by eliminating different cultures. Thus, nineteenth-century colonialism and twentieth-century militarism have given way to a twenty-first-century movement toward cultural homogeneity. Eastern Catholics, who continually fight a similar tendency in the Church, seem well suited to witness to a better form of unity for humanity. Those seeking to preserve a diversity of world cultures in a world committed to universal brotherhood need to see such a vision at work in the Church.

No one local church, however, can give that witness as effectively as many working together. Eastern Catholic leaders are challenged to increase their cooperation with one another in common charitable and mission projects on eparchial and regional levels to make the Church's unity in diversity visible in action as well as word.

Notes

1. Alexander Schmemann, "Problems of Orthodoxy in America II: The Liturgical Problem," *St. Vladimir's Seminary Quarterly* 8, no. 4 (1964), 164–85.

2. Alexander Schmemann, "Problems of Orthodoxy in America III: The Spiritual Problem," *St. Vladimir's Seminary Quarterly* 9, no. 4 (1965), 171–93.

3. See 1 Corinthians 2:6.

4. John Paul II, Apostolic Letter on the Eastern Churches, *Orientale Lumen* (Vatican City, 1995), no. 9.

5. Anaphora, Byzantine Liturgy of Saint Basil.

6. Catherine Doherty, *My Russian Yesterdays* (Milwaukee: Bruce Publishing Co., 1951), 12.

7. Joseph Tawil, *The Courage to Be Ourselves* (Newton, MA: Melkite Exarchate, 1971), 2.

Chapter 6

RELATIONS WITH OUR SISTER CHURCHES

THE EASTERN CATHOLIC WITNESS TO HISTORIC CHRISTIANITY

The pastor of an Orthodox parish in a growing suburb with a beautiful Byzantine-style church on a major thoroughfare speaks apologetically about his parish's reputation in the community. "Everyone in the area knows our church," he reveals, "but only for its Big Fat Greek Festival!"

Many Eastern Christians came to the United States as a result of oppression or discrimination in their homelands. These circumstances made an Eastern Christian presence possible where there was none before. But what does their witness contribute to Christian life in the United States? Of what do they speak to other Christians or to the community at large? Did God transplant them to the West merely in order to make specialty foods available in the suburbs? Or is their presence capable of making another statement in our world today?

The Eastern Witness at Vatican II

The vast majority of Roman Catholic bishops in the world got their first taste of the Eastern Churches at Vatican II.

Over the course of the council they participated in the Liturgy of every Eastern Catholic community whose bishops attended the deliberations. They heard the witness of a number of Eastern Catholic hierarchs on a variety of subjects. Foremost among them was the Melkite Greek Catholic Patriarch of Antioch, Maximos IV, who challenged the dominance over the Catholic Church by European and particularly curial authorities. His refusal to speak Latin, the official language of the council, because it was not the language of his Catholic Church, only of the Roman Church, was another graphic witness that the Church's true universality is found in the multiplicity of its traditions rather than in an imposed uniformity of practice. The testimony of his person and the theology from which he and other Eastern Catholic bishops spoke won the respect of many at the council, both participants and observers.

Jesuit scholar Robert F. Taft lucidly describes the impact made by Eastern Catholics at Vatican II. Western Catholics, he observed, experienced Eastern Catholics to be a bridge that allowed the voice of the East to be heard at the council sessions.

The witness of fewer than two hundred Eastern Catholic bishops, Taft remarked, exerted an influence on the twenty-five hundred Western bishops at the council far in excess of their number:

> In addition to being among the first to state categorically that the Council should avoid definitions and condemnations, the list of important items of general import on the Vatican II and post-conciliar agenda that the Melkite bishops first proposed is simply astonishing: the vernacular, eucharistic concelebration and communion under both species in the Latin liturgy; the permanent diaconate; the establishment of what

ultimately became the Synod of Bishops held periodically in Rome, as well as the Secretariat (now Pontifical Council) for Christian Unity; new attitudes and a less offensive ecumenical vocabulary for dealing with other Christians, especially with the Orthodox Churches; the recognition and acceptance of Eastern Catholic communities for what they are, "Churches," not "rites."[1]

In addition, the Eastern witness was instrumental in the reintroduction of several other liturgical elements: the prayers of the faithful and the offertory procession in the Roman Mass, baptism by immersion and the increasing administration of confirmation in conjunction with baptism as well as the entire Rite of Christian Initiation for Adults (RCIA) process, which restored a number of patristic-era elements preserved in various Eastern Churches. When the Eastern Catholic Churches gave a faithful and authentic witness to the liturgical tradition of the first millennium, it had an effect. At the same time, the spirit of renewal the council began has enabled many of these Churches to eliminate some of the careless practices that had become common in the more recent past.

The example of many Eastern Catholic Churches has led to a changed perception of the Orthodox and other Eastern Churches among Roman Catholics. Writing to the council's Central Preparatory Commission in 1961, Patriarch Maximos IV characterized the West's approach to the Orthodox in these words:

Until now the repeated and stirring calls to union that the popes addressed to our separated brethren simply hardened them more, for these calls always implied more or less the following idea: return to the sheepfold that you have abandoned, acknowledge your faults and your errors, submit, ask forgiveness, and we are ready to welcome you warmly, to hold our arms out to you, to embrace you, etc. Our Orthodox brethren are all the more astonished at this language inasmuch as they are sincerely convinced of having innovated nothing, of having remained faithful to the tradition of the days before the ruptures, and inasmuch as they believe that it is rather the Catholic Church that has strayed from apostolic tradition.[2]

As Father Taft noted, the patriarch continued to criticize the use of terms like *dissidents* and *schismatics* in the drafts of council documents and promoted the simple use of the word *Orthodox*. As he wrote in a memorandum to the Central Commission the following year, "Charity requires of us to call everyone by the name that he wishes."[3] Roman Catholic recognition of all Eastern Christians as "sister Churches," which followed in subsequent years, was built upon this witness.

Perhaps the most important witness given by the Eastern Churches, Catholic and Orthodox, to the West has been in affirming the place of first-millennium theology, spirituality, and other practices in Christian life today. Long derided as corrupt and even idolatrous by Western Christians, the Eastern tradition has achieved a measure of appreciation in the West through the Orthodox presence in the World Council of Churches and the Eastern Catholic presence at Vatican II. These led to the many bilateral dialogues between Churches and Christian communities that have characterized the years since Vatican II.

The Continuing Need for an Eastern Catholic Voice

To what degree has the witness of Eastern Catholics continued to affect Westerners? The overwhelming number of Western Catholics in contrast to the size of Eastern Catholic communities means that the Eastern witness, while no longer held in contempt, is often overlooked. The West as a rule respects the East, but in many cases still does not see it as an equal voice. When the first draft of what became the *Catechism of the Catholic Church* appeared, Eastern Catholics were surprised that, some years after Vatican II, such a document was based on a Western text, the Apostles' Creed, which is not used in any Eastern tradition. The Eastern Catholic bishops in the United States issued a common response to the draft, which reads in part:

> We submit that the Catechism works from the perspective of the Roman view throughout. Despite the fact that it incorporates an Eastern—almost exclusively Byzantine—witness to many points in the text, the CUC[4] puts them in the context of current Roman practice rather than the living context of the Eastern Churches themselves. It is, therefore, still operating from one particular tradition. In doing so, it is in fact reverting to the above-mentioned stance of seeing the Roman tradition as the principle of universality, normative for all the Churches.[5]

After a lengthy commentary on specific sections of the draft, the bishops' response concluded, "The only course of action which would not offend Eastern Catholics and not a few Orthodox would be to identify the text as a catechism, not of the Universal Church, but of the Roman Church." When the final text of the catechism appeared, the word *Universal* was deleted from the title, but there was no indication that the work was based on only one Catholic tradition. In fact, two-thirds of the Eastern references in the first draft were deleted in the final version. As a result, the Byzantine Catholic bishops in the United States resolved to issue a catechism drawn from their own tradition and began publishing the three-volume *Light for Life* to present the Byzantine perspective of their Churches. The work has since been translated into several languages for the use of Eastern Catholics in Europe and South America.

Catholic Dialogues with the Eastern Churches

As 1054 has long been a landmark date in charting the separation of Rome and Constantinople, 1964 has come to mark a new beginning in relations between the Eastern Orthodox and Roman Catholic Churches. In that year, Pope Paul VI and the Ecumenical Patriarch, Athenagoras I, finally and formally nullified the anathemas of 1054. This was the first in a series of encounters between these Churches, such as the annual joint celebration of the feasts of Saints Peter and Paul, patrons of the Roman Church, and of Saint Andrew, patron of the Church of Constantinople, as well as the return by Rome of several relics taken from the East over the years. After several years of preparation, the Joint International Commission for Theological Dialogue between these Churches was established (1980). Over the years agreed statements were produced on the mystery of the Church and the sacraments, particularly the Eucharist and holy orders.

Tensions occasioned by the revival of the Greek Catholic Churches in Eastern Europe occasioned the development of the 1993 Balamand Statement on Uniatism, cited in chapter 1. The next session of this consultation, meeting in Emmitsburg, Maryland (2000), proposed to study the "Ecclesiological and Canonical Implications of Uniatism." The session ended without resolution, as the Orthodox participants sought to revisit the concept of Orthodox and Catholics as "sister churches" and insisted on "resolving" the Uniate question before proceeding to other issues. Eastern Catholics, they felt, should either become Roman Catholics or return to the Orthodox Church. This seems to contradict the position of the Balamand Statement, which reads in part, "Concerning the Oriental Catholic Churches, it is clear that they, as part of the Catholic Communion, have the right to exist and to act in answer to the spiritual needs of their faithful."[6] The Catholic co-chairman of the dialogue, Edward Cardinal Cassidy, also noted that some Orthodox participants had had difficulty "tolerating" the presence of a Romanian Greek Catholic bishop at the talks.

Eastern Catholics, on the other hand, expressed dissatisfaction at their lack of representation on the commission. As Ukrainian Greek Catholic Bishop Basil Losten of Stamford, Connecticut, noted in a letter to Cardinal Cassidy:

> Churches have the right to speak for themselves. Since no member of the Joint International Commission for the Theological Dialogue between the Orthodox Churches and the Catholic Church has been commissioned for this purpose by any Eastern Catholic Synod or Council of Hierarchs, no such person may speak on behalf of the Eastern Catholic *sui iuris* Churches. Such a situation is not conducive to a peaceful reception of the dialogue process.[7]

In the United States, dialogue has proceeded more readily and somewhat more easily. Fifteen years before the international commission was established, the first Orthodox-Catholic Theological Consultation in the United States was held (1965). Over the years it has produced more than a score of agreed statements. While this dialogue group concentrates on theological questions, a second, composed of Orthodox and Catholic bishops, has devoted itself to considering pastoral issues.

Eastern Catholic participation in dialogue with the Eastern Orthodox is more extensive in North America than at the international level. One of the eight Catholics on the bishops' committee is a Greek Catholic. Likewise, there are several Greek Catholics on the North American Theological Consultation. There is a greater Eastern Catholic presence on the international dialogue with the Oriental Orthodox Churches. Armenian, Coptic, Ethiopian, Maronite, Syriac, and St. Thomas Catholics are members of this commission.

There have been bilateral dialogues between the Catholic Church and the various Oriental Orthodox Churches since the 1970s. In 1998, the Coptic Pope Shenouda III, the Syrian Patriarch Mar Zakka I Iwas, and the Armenian Catholicos of Cilicia Aram I agreed not to undertake dialogues with other Churches and ecclesial communions unless this could be done jointly. Accordingly a single Joint International Dialogue between the Catholic and Oriental Orthodox Churches was begun. In the United States, the first Oriental Orthodox-Catholic Consultation was held in 1978 and has produced several reports, chiefly on pastoral issues.

A Joint Committee for Theological Dialogue was established in 1994 between the Assyrian Church of the East and the Catholic Churches. It has produced a joint Christological declaration and is preparing a common declaration on the sacramental life. Most of the Catholic participants have been drawn from the Eastern Catholic Churches, including

Melkite Archbishop Cyril Boustros and Chaldean Bishop Sarhad Jammo, who serve eparchies in the United States.

Progress in this dialogue provided the incentive for practical cooperation between the Assyrian Church of the East and the Chaldean Catholic Church. In 1997, at the recommendation of both patriarchs, the synods of both Churches committed themselves to several programs, including:

> Close collaboration in the area of catechesis, particularly in training of catechists and in the development of related teaching material...[and] in the preparation and printing of liturgical books...The establishment of an ecclesial education institute in the Chicago-Detroit region, and possibly wherever members of both communities exist, for the purpose of training future priests, deacons and catechists from both Churches...The development of pastoral programs and educational projects as expressions of ecclesial and cultural collaboration between the two churches.[8]

At the same time, the two Churches established a "Joint Commission for Unity" for the purpose of achieving full ecclesiastical unity, while recognizing the need to preserve the "freedom and self-governance" of the Assyrian Church of the East and the Chaldean Church's full communion with Rome.

Two Views of Primacy

The most recent incident affecting the Catholic-Orthodox dialogue came in 2006. In that year Pope Benedict XVI discontinued using the title Patriarch of the West to avoid any suggestion of Euro-centrism in the modern Catholic Church. Eastern Christians, however, both Catholic and Orthodox, reacted negatively. In a formal expression of concern, the Holy Synod of the Ecumenical Patriarchate noted that Patriarch of the West was "the only [papal title] that goes back to the period of the Undivided Church of the first millennium, and which has been accepted in the conscience of the Orthodox Church.[9] Abolishing it while retaining other titles such as "Supreme Pontiff," the Synod observed, creates "serious difficulties"[10] for the Orthodox who see the move as another instance of the pope's claim to universal jurisdiction over all the Churches. The Synod stressed that Orthodox ecclesiology is based on the communion of local Churches. It accepts the idea that the bishop of one local Church have precedence in a metropolia, a patriarchate, or in the universal Church, but that he still remains primarily bishop of a local Church.

In response, a curia official described as "familiar with the dialogue" told Cindy Wooden of the Catholic News Service that the Vatican did not believe dropping the title would have a negative impact on the dialogue or on moves to restore full communion between Catholics and Orthodox. He noted that the bishop of Rome exercises his primacy differently over the Latin-rite Church and with the Eastern Catholic Churches, as seen in the two codes of canon law. This, he said, "leaves open possibilities for the future of differing relationships, although communion with the bishop of Rome remains essential.[11]

Citing the Roman code for Eastern Catholics as a model stands in stark contrast to the Balamand Statement's insistence that "...'uniatism' can no longer be accepted...as a model of the unity our Churches are seeking."[12] Eastern Catholic hierarchs and canonists need to witness clearly to these anomalies in Catholic understanding and practice vis-a-vis the relationship of the Churches.

Eastern Catholics also noted that, while the pope seemed

to indicate that the Western Church shouold not be identified solely with Western Europe, the Vatican continues to insist that the jurisdiction of Eastern Catholic patriarchs and primates be restricted to their "historic territory," even though their Churches too are now established throughout the world.

A different sense of primacy was expressed in the crisis affecting the autocephalous Orthodox Church of Cyprus. Its chief hierarch, Archbishop Chrysostomos, has been suffering for four years from the irreversible effects of Alzheimer's disease. The Cypriot Church had no canons addressing what should be done when a hierarch is permanently disabled in this way. Its synod of bishops, unable to agree on a course of action, appealed to the ecumenical patriarch, who in May, 2006 summoned a "Greater Synod," including the Cypriot bishops and the patriarchs of the apostolic sees (the pentarchy). It was this synod that declared the archiepiscopal See vacant and began the process for electing a new archbishop.

Grassroots Cooperation

Ecumenical progress on the levels mentioned has encouraged cooperation by eparchies of various Eastern Churches in the United States. These efforts to date have been between Churches that were previously one. Since 2003, the Ukrainian Orthodox and Greek Catholic bishops in North America have held a series of "Fraternal Encounters" in which they discussed issues of common interest. They designated a common day of prayer to remember victims of the forced famine of 1932–1933 in the Soviet Union. The bishops laid plans for a common conference of their respective clergy and a program of common prayer services in one another's Churches. A joint commission has since begun work on developing a program of family catechesis to bring together members of both Churches on a regular basis.

For several years the Ruthenian Greek Catholic eparchy of Pittsburgh, in cooperation with the Carpatho-Russian Orthodox Diocese headquartered in Johnstown, Pennsylvania, has sponsored an annual Spirituality Conference, for the clergy and faithful of both jurisdictions. Students and staff of their respective seminaries have exchanged visits to develop appreciation of one another's Churches. As in other jurisdictions, grassroots cooperation has depended on the initiative of local clergy.

Addressing the need for pastoral cooperation, Pope John Paul II wrote:

> The Eastern Catholic Bishops will not neglect any means of encouraging an atmosphere of brotherhood, sincere mutual esteem and co-operation with their brothers in the Churches with which we are not yet united in full communion, especially with those who belong to the same ecclesial tradition.[13]

His words are a continual reminder of the need to develop fraternal exchanges among all the Eastern Churches.

John Paul's call to share was not limited to the Eastern Churches alone. He urged the Churches of East and West to develop relationships:

> It is important that meetings and exchanges should involve Church communities in the broadest forms and ways. We know for example how positive interparish activities such as "twinning" can be for mutual cultural and spiritual enrichment, and also for the exercise of charity.[14]

One type of interparish exchange that has been suggested is the "Encounter Weekend" in which parishioners are invited to a church of a different tradition. Talks and workshops, perhaps on Saturday, would familiarize visitors with the background and practices of the host parish. Members of both parishes would have the opportunity to interact, perhaps over a meal. Attendance at the host parish's Sunday liturgy would conclude the encounter.

The presence of so many of the historic Eastern Churches in North America provides the opportunity for Eastern and Western Christians to interact in unprecedented ways. To the degree that this is realized what was envisioned in the pope's 1995 Apostolic Letter quoted previously will be fulfilled. It seems appropriate to conclude these pages with some final words from the papal letter:

> The words of the West need the words of the East, so that God's word may ever more clearly reveal its unfathomable riches. Our words will meet forever in the heavenly Jerusalem, but we ask and wish that this meeting be anticipated in the holy Church which is still on her way towards the fullness of the Kingdom.[15]

Notes

1. Unpublished preface to *The Melkite Greek Church at the Council,* translation of *L'Eglise Grecque Melkite au Councile* (Beirut: Dar al-Kalima, 1967).

2. *L'Eglise,* chap. 12, "Ecumenism: The Requirements for Union."

3. Ibid.

4. Catechism of the Universal Church, the original working title.

5. Eastern Catholic Bishops in the United States, Response to the Universal Catechism (unpublished document).

6. Joint International Commission for the Theological Dialogue between the Roman Catholic Church and the Orthodox

Church, "Uniatism, Method of Union of the Past, and the Present Search for Full Communion," no. 12, in *Eastern Churches Journal* 1, no. 3 (1993).

7. *Ukrainian Weekly,* July 16, 2000, vol. XLVIII, no. 29.

8. "Joint Synodal Decree for Promoting Unity" (1997), no. 4.

9. *Announcement of the Chief Secretary of the Holy and Sacred Synod regarding the denouncement by Pope Benedict XVI of Rome of the title "Patriarch of the West,"* June 8, 2006, no. 2.

10. Ibid. no. 5.

11. Cindy Wooden, "Orthodox express concern about dropping 'patriarch of the West' title" (Catholic News Service, June 13, 2006).

12. Op. cit. no. 12: For one view of how "different" the Eastern Code of Canons is, see pages 35–37, above.

13. John Paul II, Apostolic Letter to Mark the Centenary of *Orientalium Dignitas* by Pope Leo XIII, *Orientale Lumen* (Vatican City, 1995), no. 26.

14. Ibid., no. 25.

15. Ibid., no. 28.

Appendix A

THE EASTERN CATHOLIC CHURCHES IN NORTH AMERICA

The Armenian Church

Eparchy of Our Lady of Nareg in New York
167 North Sixth Street
Brooklyn, NY 11211

> Serving Armenian Catholics throughout the United States and Canada, with parishes in the states of California, Massachusetts, Michigan, New Jersey, and Pennsylvania and the provinces of Ontario and Quebec.

Contact: 718/388-4218 (voice); 718/486-0615 (fax); mbexarch@aol.com (e-mail)

The Byzantine Churches

1. *The Melkite Greek Catholic Church*

Eparchy of Newton
3 VFW Parkway
Roslindale, MA 02131

> Serving Melkites throughout the United States with parishes in Alabama, Arizona, California, Connecticut, Florida, Georgia, Illinois, Indiana, Louisiana,

Massachusetts, Michigan, New Hampshire, New Jersey, New York, Ohio, Pennsylvania, Rhode Island, South Carolina, Virginia, Washington, and Wisconsin.

Web site: www.melkite.org

Contact: 617/323-9922 (voice); 617/323-0188 (fax); eparchyofnewton@msn.com (e-mail)

Eparchy of Saint Sauveur de Montreal
34 Maplewood Avenue
Outremont, Quebec H2V 2M1

Serving Melkites throughout Canada with parishes in British Columbia, Ontario, and Quebec.

Web site: www.melkite.com

Contact: 514/272-6430 (voice); 514/272-2341 (fax); eparchie.st-sauveur@bellnet.ca (e-mail)

2. The Romanian Greek Catholic Church

Eparchy of Canton
1121 44th Street NE
Canton, OH 44714

Serving Romanian Greek Catholics throughout the United States with parishes in California, Illinois, Indiana, Massachusetts, Michigan, New Jersey, New York, Ohio, and Pennsylvania.

Web site: www.romaniancatholic.org

Contact: 330/492-4086 (voice); 330/493-1416 (fax); omarginean@romaniancatholic.org (e-mail)

3. The (Ruthenian) Byzantine Catholic Church

Archeparchy of Pittsburgh
66 Riverview Avenue
Pittsburgh, PA 15214

> Serving Byzantine Catholics with parishes in Louisiana, eastern Ohio, Oklahoma, western Pennsylvania, Tennessee, Texas, and West Virginia.

Web site: www.archeparchy.org

Contact: 412/231-4000 (voice); 412/231-1697 (fax); communications@archeparchy.org (e-mail)

Eparchy of Parma
1900 Carlton Road
Parma, OH 44134

> Serving Byzantine Catholics with parishes in Illinois, Indiana, Michigan, Minnesota, Missouri, and Ohio.

Web site: www.parma.org

Contact: 216/741-8773 (voice); 216/742-9356 (fax); viscom@parma.org (e-mail)

Eparchy of Passaic
445 Lackawanna Avenue
West Paterson, NJ 07424

> Serving Byzantine Catholics in the eastern United States, with parishes in Connecticut, Florida, Georgia, Massachusetts, Maryland, New Jersey, New York, North Carolina, eastern Pennsylvania, and Virginia.

Web site: www.dreamwater.org/edu/passaic

Contact: 973/890-7777 (voice); 973/890-7175 (fax)

Eparchy of Van Nuys
8105 North 16th Street
Phoenix, AZ 85020

> Serving Byzantine Catholics in the western United States, with parishes in Alaska, Arizona, California, Colorado, Nebraska, New Mexico, Oregon, and Washington.

Web site: www.eparchy-of-van-nuys.org

Contact: 602/861-9778 (voice); 602/861-9796 (fax); evnsecretary@gwest.net (e-mail)

Slovak Eparchy of Saints Cyril and Methodius
223 Carlton Road
Unionville, Ontario L3R 3M2

> Serving Slovak Byzantine Catholics throughout Canada, with parishes in Alberta, British Columbia, Manitoba, Ontario, Quebec, and Saskatchewan.

Contact: 905/477-4867 (voice); 905/479-9629 (fax); byzslovakeparch@sympatico.ca (e-mail)

4. The Ukrainian Greek Catholic Church

Archeparchy of Philadelphia
827 North Franklin Street
Philadelphia, PA 19123

> Serving Ukrainian Greek Catholics in the east central United States, with parishes in Delaware, the District of Columbia, Maryland, New Jersey, eastern Pennsylvania, and Virginia.

Web site: www.ukrarcheparchy.com

Contact: 215/627-0143 (voice); 215/627-0377 (fax); ukrmet@catholic.org (e-mail)

Eparchy of Saint Josaphat in Parma
P.O. Box 347180
Parma, OH 44134

> Serving Ukrainian Greek Catholics in the central and southern United States, with parishes in Florida, Georgia, Ohio, western Pennsylvania, and West Virginia.

Web site: www.stjosaphateparchy.org

Contact: 216/888-1522 (voice); 216/888-3477 (fax)

Eparchy of Saint Nicholas in Chicago
2245 West Rice Street
Chicago, IL 60622

> Serving Ukrainian Greek Catholics in the western United States, with parishes in Arizona, California, Colorado, Hawaii, Illinois, Indiana, Kansas, Mississippi, Minnesota, Missouri, Nebraska, North Dakota, Oregon, Texas, Washington, and Wisconsin.

Web site: www.stnicholaseparchy.org

Contact: 773/276-8080 (voice); 773/276-6799 (fax); sneparchy@iols.com (e-mail)

Eparchy of Stamford
14 Peveril Road
Stamford, CT 06902

> Serving Ukrainian Greek Catholics in the eastern United States, with parishes in Connecticut, Massachusetts, New Hampshire, New York, and Rhode Island.

Web site: www.stamforddio.org

Contact: 203/324-7896 (voice); 203/967-9948 (fax); stamfordeparchy@optonline.net (e-mail)

Archeparchy of Winnipeg
233 Scotia Street
Winnipeg, Manitoba R2V 1V7

> Serving Ukrainian Greek Catholics with parishes in the province of Manitoba.

Web site: www.archeparchy.ca

Contact: 204/338-7801 (voice); 204/339-4006 (fax)

Eparchy of Edmonton
9645 108th Avenue
Edmonton, Alberta T5H 1A3

> Serving Ukrainian Greek Catholics with parishes in the province of Alberta.

Web site: www.edmontoneparchy.com

Contact: 780/424-5496 (voice); 780/425-2333 (fax); chancery@edmontoneparchy.com (e-mail)

Eparchy of New Westminster
502 Fifth Avenue
New Westminster, British Columbia V3L 1S2

> Serving Ukrainian Greek Catholics with parishes in the province of British Columbia, the Yukon Territory, and the Northwest Territories.

Web site: www.vcn.bc.ca

Contact: 604/524-8824 (voice); 604/521-8015 (fax); bsy.osbm@telus.net (e-mail)

Eparchy of Saskatoon
866 Saskatchewan Crescent East
Saskatoon, Saskatchewan S7N 0L4

Serving Ukrainian Greek Catholics with parishes in the province of Saskatchewan.

Web site: www.skeparchy.com

Contact: 306/653-0138 (voice); 306/665-2569 (fax); admin.skeparchy@sassktel.net (e-mail)

Eparchy of Toronto and Eastern Canada
940 The East Mall, Suite #201
Toronto, Ontario M9B 6J7

Serving Ukrainian Greek Catholics in eastern Canada with parishes in the provinces of Nova Scotia, Ontario, and Quebec.

Web site: www.ucet.ca

Contact: 416/7460154 (voice); 416/746-6003 (fax); eparchto@bellnet.ca (e-mail)

The Syriac Churches

5. The Chaldean Catholic Church

Eparchy of Saint Peter
1627 Jamacha Way
El Cajon, CA 92019

Serving Chaldean Catholics in the western United States, with parishes in Arizona, California, and Nevada.

Contact: 619/579-7913 (voice); 619/588-8281 (fax)

Eparchy of Saint Thomas the Apostle
25585 Berg Road
Southfield, MI 48076

Serving Chaldean Catholics in the eastern United States, with parishes in Illinois and Michigan.

Web site: www.chaldeandiocese.org

Contact: 248/351-0440 (voice); 248/351-0443 (fax); secretary@chaldeandiocese.org (e-mail)

6. The Maronite Church

Eparchy of Our Lady of Lebanon
1021 South Tenth Street
St. Louis, MO 63104

Serving Maronite Catholics in the western United States, with parishes in Alabama, Arizona, California, Colorado, Illinois, Michigan, Minnesota, Nevada, Ohio, Oklahoma, Oregon, Texas, Utah, Washington, and West Virginia.

Web site: www.usamaronite.org

Contact: 314/231-1021 (voice); 314/231-1418 (fax); joan@usamaronite.org (e-mail)

Eparchy of Saint Maron of Brooklyn
109 Remsen Street
Brooklyn, NY 11201

Serving Maronite Catholics in the eastern United States, with parishes in Connecticut, the District of Columbia, Florida, Georgia, Maine, Massachusetts, New Hampshire, New Jersey, New York, North Carolina, Pennsylvania, Rhode Island, South Carolina, and Virginia.

Web site: www.stmaron.org

Contact: 718/237-9913 (voice); 718/243-0444 (fax)

7. The Syriac Catholic Church

Eparchy of Our Lady of Deliverance
502 Palisade Avenue, P.O. Box 8366
Union City, NJ 07087

> Serving Syriac Catholics throughout the United States and Canada, with parishes in the states of Arizona, California, Florida, Michigan, New Jersey, Pennsylvania, and Rhode Island, and in the provinces of Ontario and Quebec.

Web site: www.syriac-catholic.org

Contact: 201/683-1067 (voice); 201/683-0212 (fax); frsyriac@aol.com (e-mail)

8. The Syro-Malabar Catholic Church

St. Thomas Diocese of Chicago
3009 South 49th Avenue
Cicero, IL 60804

> Serving Syro-Malabarese Catholics in thirty-three parishes throughout the United States and Canada.

Web site: www.stthomasdiocese.org

Contact: 708/656-3362 (voice); 708/656-8663 (fax); kaduppilroy@yahoo.com (e-mail)

9. The Syro-Malankara Catholic Church

Mar Ivanios Malankara Catholic Center
905 Hillside Avenue
New Hyde Park, NY 11040

> Coordinating the activities of Syro-Malankarese Catholics throughout the United States and Canada,

with parishes in the District of Columbia, in the states of Georgia, Illinois, Michigan, New Jersey, New York, Pennsylvania, and Texas, and in the province of Ontario.

Web site: www.malankara.net North America

Contact: 516/258-6905 (voice); 516/616-0727 (fax)

Organizations

10. Eastern Catholic Associates

The association of Eastern Catholic hierarchs includes all the bishops of the eparchies in the United States listed previously. Its catechetical committee is the Eastern Catholic Diocesan Directors of Religious Education (ECDD) and its publishing arm is God With Us Publications.

Web site: www.ecdd.org

Contact: gwupub@juno.com

Appendix B

A COMPARISON
OF TWO TRADITIONS

In Liturgy

Western Tradition

Model for the Mass is the Lord's Supper, reflecting beauty in simplicity with clear messages, frugal use of symbols, and a focus on the here and now. Prayers are straightforward and direct, with little repetition. Reading alternates with silence, popular nonliturgical hymns or instrumental music as a background to reflection. The worshiping community gathers with the priest around the Lord's Table to celebrate His presence with us now.

Byzantine Tradition

Model for the Divine Liturgy is the heavenly liturgy, with a focus on eschatology (that is, heaven on earth) and the fullness of God-life, expressed in continual singing of the liturgical texts, and repetition as way to communion with the Lord God. Much movement and appeal to the senses are meant to get the whole self (mind and body) involved in worship. The priest and community stand together facing East, whence Christ will come again.

In Thought and Expression

Western Tradition

More linear, often preferring juridical or philosophical clarity to poetic synthesis. The theology of the Trinity emphasizes the oneness of God in three persons. Reflection on or devotion to Christ stresses his humanity: Jesus of Nazareth. The Blessed Virgin Mary, Mother of Jesus, is Our Lady, Mother, and Queen, whose intercession with Christ on our behalf is the focus of devotion. The "permanent and visible source and foundation" of the Church's unity is found in Christ's vicar, the pope, the "bishop of the Catholic Church." The model of Christian living is Christ's humanity: we strive to live as he did.

Byzantine Tradition

More symbolic, preferring poetic synthesis and paradox to philosophical analysis. The theology of the Trinity emphasizes the Father, Son, and Holy Spirit, one God. Reflection on and devotion to Christ stress his divinity: the Lord of Glory. The Holy Virgin is Theotokos, she who bore God, whose place at the head of all creation because of her role in the incarnation is emphasized. The Holy Spirit is the guarantor of a Church's unity, visibly expressed through the communion of local churches. The model of Christian living is the mutual love of the Trinity in whose image we are created as a people meant for communion.

In Church Art and Architecture

Western Tradition

No one preferred style: many different approaches help us express what God's love means for us. Contemporary artists are encouraged to let their individual experience of God come through their art, encouraging creativity and artistic freedom. Church buildings are primarily gathering places for the worshiping community, with little adornment. Focus is on the altar and the cross, images of Christ's sacrifice.

Byzantine Tradition

Icons express the Church's teaching in the reality of the incarnation and the transforming power of the Holy Spirit. The individual artist's ideas are secondary, and iconographers are expected to follow traditional forms for expressing the Church's faith. The church building is an icon of the Church, the communion of saints, with many icons, focused on the icon of Christ, Ruler of All, who will come again.

SOME BASIC RESOURCES

For an overview of the origins and organization of all the Eastern Churches, including the Old Believers and Old Calendarist Churches, see

Ronald Roberson, *The Eastern Christian Churches: A Brief Survey,* 6th ed. (Rome: Edizioni Orientalia Christiani, Pontifical Oriental Institute, 1999).

Father Roberson regularly presents an extensive, updated survey of news in various Eastern Churches in the periodical *Eastern Churches Journal* (Fairfax, VA: Eastern Christian Publications).

For an introduction to the spiritual and liturgical tradition of the Byzantine Churches, Orthodox and Catholic, see

Lawrence Cross, *Eastern Christianity: The Byzantine Tradition* (Sydney and Philadelphia: E J Dwyer, 1988), and

John Meyendorff, *Byzantine Theology* (New York: Fordham University Press, 1979).

A comparable introduction to the tradition of the Syriac Churches is

Seely J. Beggiani, *Introduction to Eastern Christian Spirituality: The Syriac Tradition* (Scranton, PA: University of Scranton Press, 1991).

Information on all the Eastern Churches from A to Z (literally) may be found in *The Blackwell Dictionary of Eastern Christianity* (Oxford, UK, and Malden, MA: Blackwell, 1999).

A pastoral presentation of the Byzantine tradition commissioned by the Byzantine Catholic bishops in the United States may be found in the three volumes of

Light for Life (Pittsburgh: God With Us Publications): *The Mystery Believed* (1994), *The Mystery Celebrated* (1996), and *The Mystery Lived* (2001).

For an overview of the Maronite tradition based on its liturgical cycle, see

Anthony J. Salim, *Captivated by Your Teachings* (Tucson: E T Nedder, 2002).

A 1927 study of the difference between Church unity and Uniatism remains a good summary of the subject. See

Cyril Korolevsky, *Uniatism: Definition, Causes, Effects, Scope, Dangers, Remedies,* trans. Serge Keleher (Fairfax, VA: Eastern Christian Publications, 2001).

For documents generated in the Eastern Orthodox-Catholic dialogue, see

John Borelli and John H. Erickson, eds., *The Quest for Unity: Orthodox and Catholics in Dialogue* (Crestwood, NY: St. Vladimir's Seminary Press and Washington, DC: United States Catholic Conference, 1996).

The writings of Joseph Raya and Robert Taft, available from various publishers, present aspects of the Byzantine tradition on several levels. A principal source on the Syriac tradition is the work of Sebastian Brock, particularly his three-volume *The Hidden Pearl,* prepared in cooperation with the Syriac Orthodox Church.

More extensive listings of basic Eastern Catholic publications may be found in the catalogs of

Eastern Christian Publications (P.O. Box 146, Fairfax, VA 22030)

God With Us Publications (P.O. Box 99203, Pittsburgh, PA 15233) and

Sophia Press (3 VFW Parkway, Roslindale, MA 02131).

Significant Orthodox publishers in the United States include
Conciliar Press (P.O. Box 76, Ben Lomond, CA 95005)

Light and Life Publishing (4818 Park Glen Road, Minneapolis, MN 55416)

St. Vladimir's Seminary Press (575 Scarsdale Road, Crestwood, NY 10707)

The publications of individual Eastern Church jurisdictions, including their liturgical texts, are generally available from the headquarters of each jurisdiction.

Web sites of some Eastern Churches contain a great deal of information. The sites of many Eastern Churches may be accessed through www.byzcath.org.

SELECTED GLOSSARY

Autocephalous Church In current Orthodox usage, a Church is autocephalous ("its own head") when it is in no way dependent on any outside authority. There are today no autocephalous Churches in the Catholic communion.

Autonomous Church In current Orthodox usage, a Church is autonomous ("with its own laws") when it is dependent on a mother Church, usually for the selection of its primate (or bishops). All the Eastern Catholic Churches are autonomous Churches (Latin: *sui juris*).

Archbishop In Greek Churches an archbishop is the head of an autocephalous Church (for example, Greece) or an autonomous Church (for example, Sinai). In Slavic use the term is an honorary title given to meritorious bishops. In some Eastern Catholic Churches, the term is used for all ruling bishops and the title "archbishop major" (senior archbishop) is used for the head of the Church.

Catholicate The jurisdiction of a catholicos.

Catholicos The title of the head of the Armenian, Assyrian/Chaldean, Georgian, and Syro-Malankara Churches.

Ecumenical Council In origin, a council of all the bishops of the *ecumene* (that is, the entire Roman/Byzantine Empire), summoned by the emperor to promote unity among the Churches. Some, but not all, of the councils so designated were received by the Churches. After the separation of the Greek and Latin Churches, the term continued to be used in the West for councils called by the pope and considered *ipso* *facto* ecumenical, although many of them had exclusively Latin participation.

Ecumenical Patriarch The title assumed by the Archbishop of Constantinople in the sixth century, meaning chief bishop of the *ecumene*. Today the Ecumenical Patriarch is considered the "first among equals" in the hierarchy of the Eastern Orthodox Churches.

Eikonostasis or **iconostasis** The screen or wall between the holy place (sanctuary) and nave in Byzantine and Coptic churches. Adorned with icons connected with the mystery of our salvation, it represents the union of God and humanity accomplished in Christ. It is pierced by three doorways for the passage of the clergy and their attendants during certain liturgical services.

Eparchy Greek term for a diocese, originally taken from Roman civil administration.

Epiclesis A prayer invoking the transforming presence and operation of the Holy Spirit. There are epicleses in the Divine Liturgy, the Great Blessing of Water, and other sacramental rites in various Eastern Churches.

Equal to the Apostles A title given to some individuals instrumental in the evangelization of their region or nation.

Hierarch A generic title for bishops of all ranks.

In Communion Being "in communion with" Rome or Constantinople or Alexandria signifies full sacramental relationship between different local Churches. In the East it is considered the basis for the legitimacy of a local Church.

Melkite Literally, a "king's man," used originally as a slur against followers of the emperor's (Chalcedonian) faith in the Patriarchate of Antioch. Now used chiefly to refer to

Greek Catholics in the Patriarchates of Alexandria, Antioch, and Jerusalem.

Metropolia or **Metropolitanate** Province under the jurisdiction of a metropolitan.

Metropolitan In Greek Churches a metropolitan is the bishop of a metropolis, or principal city: the ruling bishop of a diocese. In Slavic use, as in the West, a metropolitan is chief bishop of an ecclesiastical province (that is, a group of dioceses).

Pantocrator Literally, "the Ruler of all," a title of Christ. The icon of Christ the Pantocrator is typically the principal icon in a Byzantine church, placed in the dome or in the apse.

Patriarch The title of the head of a number of Eastern Churches. The patriarchates of Rome, Constantinople, Alexandria, Antioch, and Jerusalem are considered Apostolic Sees because of their eparchy's connection with an apostle.

Patriarchate The jurisdiction of a patriarch.

Patristic Pertaining to a Father of the Church.

Provincial Council An occasional gathering of bishops of a metropolitan province. Local councils were common in the West before Vatican I. When there was only one Roman Catholic archdiocese in the United States, several Provincial Councils of Baltimore were held. When more archdioceses were created, Plenary Councils were held.

Synod A regular gathering of bishops in many Eastern Churches. Some synods include all the bishops or all the ruling bishops of a Church; other gatherings, called "permanent synods" involve a smaller circle of bishops chosen periodically to assist the patriarch.

Zeon In the Byzantine rite, a small amount of hot water added to the chalice before Communion with the words "The fervor of faith, filled with the Holy Spirit." The warmed chalice suggests the living body of the risen Christ.